The
Second World War
Illustrated

The Second Year

The
Second World War
Illustrated

The Second Year

J<small>ACK</small> H<small>OLROYD</small>

Pen & Sword
MILITARY

Dedicated to the One True Sovereign
To serve as a visual reminder of the consequences when
mankind persists in a course of rebellion against His rulership

First published in Great Britain in 2020 by
PEN & SWORD MILITARY
an imprint of
Pen & Sword Books Ltd,
47 Church Street, Barnsley,
South Yorkshire.
S70 2AS

Copyright © Jack Holroyd 2020

ISBN 9781526757944

The right of Jack Holroyd to be identified as Author of this Work
has been asserted by them in accordance with the
Copyright, Designs and Patents Act 1988.

A CIP catalogue record for this book is available
from the British Library

Designed by Factionpress
Printed and bound in India by Replika Press Pvt. Ltd.

Pen & Sword Books Ltd incorporates the imprints of
Pen & Sword Aviation, Pen & Sword Maritime,
Pen & Sword Military, Pen & Sword Select, Pen & Sword Military Classics,
Leo Cooper, Wharncliffe Local History

For a complete list of Pen & Sword titles please contact:
PEN & SWORD BOOKS LIMITED
47 Church Street, Barnsley, South Yorkshire, S70 2AS, England.
E-mail: enquiries@pen-and-sword.co.uk
Website: www.pen-and-sword.co.uk

Contents

Foreword

by Nigel Cave

The Second World War Illustrated – *The Second Year*

The second year was one of almost unrelieved disaster as regards the Allied cause, whilst the Germans could look back with some satisfaction on what their forces had achieved, despite some notable failings by their Italian partners. By the early summer of 1941 Great Britain was faced by a continental Europe that was even more firmly under Hitler's control than in the dark, dismal days following the evacuation from Dunkirk and the Fall of France. When German conquests are combined with the reality of the other dictatorial governments in Europe, most of which could be described as fascist in nature – for example those of Spain, Portugal and Hungary, the prospects for Britain and its Dominions by September 1941 seemed at least as bleak as they were at the same time in 1940. The one possible glimmer of light lay with the Soviet Union, brought into the fray by Hitler's invasion in late June, although it could hardly be said that the paranoid and unpredictable Stalin had been enjoying a war that was going extraordinarily badly.

British forces in campaigns outside the United Kingdom itself had been almost uniformly unsuccessful. At first there were signs of promise, however. Both in North Africa and the eastern Mediterranean, Mussolini's adventurism, in line with his belief that the sea and its adjoining territories were Italy's *mare nostra*, proved to be catastrophic. He had to be bailed out by the diversion of valuable German manpower, in North Africa notably under the capable and dynamic leadership of Erwin Rommel. Not only did Rommel stem the tide of the British advances along the Libyan coast but he turned the tables and once more British control of Egypt and of the Suez Canal was under a real threat of being lost. Similarly, Mussolini's ill-judged attacks in the Aegean in the autumn of 1940 came spectacularly unstuck and Italy was forced, once more, to turn to the Germans. Bringing on board hitherto 'neutral' nations and in a series of campaigns that bore all the characteristics of the Blitzkrieg tactics that had worked so effectively in 1940, Yugoslavia and Greece fell to the Axis powers. At the same time, Hungary and Rumania came firmly into the Axis camp. British intervention resulted in an all too similar tale of woe: outmanoeuvred, outgunned and out-generaled, the depressing photographs of captured British and Dominion soldiers from Libya to Crete were triumphantly distributed across the world's media by an exultant Goebbels, Hitler's master of propaganda.

The situation was not much better at sea – indeed the effectiveness of the German submarine campaign against the life blood of Britain's merchant shipping proved a far more immediate danger, one that was not really overcome until the winter of 1943 and never entirely suppressed. The outstanding feature of this particular campaign – the struggle to maintain supplies or to destroy them – was that it was continuous and unrelenting, a fact that has tended to obscure its achievements. Merchant ships and their passengers and cargo faced the very real prospect of being destroyed for much of their voyages – they lived in perpetual nervous tension. Their protectors, be it at sea or in the air, endured dangerous conditions and at the same time days of seemingly interminable boredom. The U boat commanders and crews fought a largely solitary war (though the use of 'wolf packs' was a feature of the campaign) in their still quite primitive boats, with their tough living conditions and the inherent perils of having a craft that was often deep underwater and so very vulnerable, ever more so as anti-submarine measures new and old became ever more effective.

The British home front for the first months of 1941 was dominated by the Blitz. Today, secure in decades of peace, it is difficult to imagine what life was like for those on the ground who faced the incessant fear of night time raids – originally concentrated on London in the latter months of 1940 and then extending to many of Britain's industrial and port cities. German night bombing might be considered to have been a success; but anti-aircraft measures, both from the ground and in the air, became increasingly successful. The German air campaign had certainly disrupted British war industry, as much because of the precautionary measures taken to ensure an acceptable as opposed to an optimum level of production as by the actual damage caused by the bombs. By May 1941 Hitler had turned his attentions and his military capacity elsewhere; so far as he was concerned, Britain had been militarily contained and could be dealt with after he had completed his 'mission' in the east.

Two major factors emerged in 1941 that were, eventually, to determine the outcome of the war. The first of these was the benevolent intervention of the United States. Franklin Roosevelt, the American President, decided to do almost anything but declare war against the Axis powers in Europe. The Lend Lease Agreement provided surplus, more or less obsolete, US Navy destroyers to the Royal Navy and there were almost limitless lines of credit for the purchase of American material. By mid 1941 the Americans provided, effectively, escorts to convoys as far as Iceland. The second was Hitler's fateful decision to invade the Soviet Union. Although the Germans made staggering territorial gains and inflicted quite extraordinarily high casualties on the Russians, they failed to deliver a knock-out blow and were soon bogged down in vicious fighting with a resolute enemy that counted no cost too great to save the Motherland.

By September 1941 there were glimmerings of hope for the British. A vital Mediterranean staging post for both sides, Malta, remained in British hands, despite the best endeavours of the Axis, in particular the Italians, to bomb it into submission. The arrival of Stalin on the British side of the war, an unlikely alliance of convenience, meant that oil-rich Persia – since 1935 to be known as Iran – became a target for them. In addition to its huge oil reserves, it would provide a conduit for British aid to the Soviets; and it would continue the British policy of securing its interests in the Middle East, most recently shown by a successful war in Iraq. The joint campaign lasted less than a month, commencing in late August, and left the country split into British and Soviet areas of influence.

By Autumn 1941 it could be said that Germany had had another successful year in the war. It had been forced by the inadequacy and ambitions of Mussolini to divert some resources – but the end result was broadly satisfactory. It had failed to subdue Britain, but that country could do little to influence matters on the continent and had, generally, rather disappointing results in areas where it did intervene, albeit one or two notable exceptions. More seriously, Britain's maritime trade was under extreme pressure. However, there were changes in the air that would at least push the balance more in Britain's favour. The first was the stalling of the German advance in Russia; the second was a pro-British USA, whose government tested the notion of neutrality almost to breaking point with its supportive policies. By December 1941 this was to be transformed into open hostilities with the attack on Pearl Harbor by the Japanese and Hitler's declaration of war on the USA.

It was to be a very different war from now on.

Nigel Cave
Ratcliffe College

Bibliography

THE STRUGGLE FOR EUROPE *by Chester Wilmot* THE REPRINT SOCIETY, 1954
THE FATAL DECISIONS *by* SIEGRFIED WESTPHAL PEN & SWORD BOOKS LTD, 2012
ROMMEL IN HIS OWN WORDS *Editor Dr John Pimlott* GREENHILL BOOKS 1994
WAFFEN-SS COMMANDERS *by Mark C Yerger* SCHIFFER MILITARY HISTORY 1997
VOLUMES 1 and 2

Battleground MALTA *by Paul Williams* PEN & SWORD BOOKS LTD, 2009

THE AXIS OCCUPATION OF EUROPE *by Winston & Gail Ramsey* AFTER THE BATTLE, 2018
THE BLITZ THEN & NOW VOLUME TWO *by Winston G Ramsey*
(AFTER THE BATTLE MAGAZINE) 2017
THE DESERT WAR THEN & NOW *by Jean Paul Pallud* AFTER THE BATTLE, 2012

THE BOMBER COMMAND WAR DIARIES 1939 - 1945
Martin Middlebrook and Chris Everitt, 2014
FAMOUS BOMBERS OF THE SECOND WORLD WAR *by William Green*
MACDONALD AND JANE'S PUBLISHERS 1979
FAMOUS FIGHTERS OF THE SECOND WORLD WAR *by William Green*
MACDONALD AND JANE'S PUBLISHERS 1977
FIGHTER SQUADRONS OF THE RAF *by John D R Rawlings* MACDONALD, LONDON 1969
THE GREAT PATRIOTIC WAR *by Peter G Tsouras* GREENHILL BOOKS, LONDON 1992
U-BOATS *by Antony Preston* ARMS & ARMOUR PRESS, LONDON 1978

PICTORIAL HISTORY OF THE WAR (FIRST YEAR SEVEN VOLUMES)
Edited by Walter Hutchinson, VIRTUE & COMPANY LTD
THE SECOND GREAT WAR (NINE VOLUMES) *Edited by Sir John Hammerton*
THE WAVERLEY BOOK COMPANY LTD
THE WAR IN PICTURES (SIX VOLUMES) ODHAMS PRESS LTD
HISTORY OF THE SECOND WORLD WAR PURNELL AND SONS LTD 1966
WORLD WAR II (TWELVE VOLUMES) *Editor Brigadier Peter Young*
ORBIS PUBLISHING LIMITED 1972

ILLUSTRIERTE GESCHICHTE DES ZWEITEN WELTTKIEGS
Kurt Zentner SÜDWEST VERLAG, MUNCHEN 1967

EIN JAHRHUNDERT UNTER WASSER
Eckard Wetzel MOTORBUCH VERLAG, STUTTGART 1916

MESSERSCHMITT BF 109 VOM PROTOTYP BIS ZUR BF 109 K
Markus Wunderlich 2017 GERAMOND VERLAG GMBH, MÜNCHEN

WENN ALLE BRÜDER SCHWEIGEN
GROSSER BILDBAND ÜBER DIE WAFFEN-SS, MUNIN-VERLAG GMBH, OSNABRUECK 1985

HISTOIRE D'UN MONDE EN GUERRE 39-45
under the direction of Claude Quétel LAROUSSE 2015

PETER TAYLOR PHOTOGRAPHIC ARCHIVE
PEN & SWORD HISTORY BOOKS

002ww2/2 New Zealand infantrymen find an Italian unit colour among abandoned food and equipment at a captured Italian position in Egypt.

Chapter One: **Mussolini Invades Egypt**

001ww2/2 Italian pilots planning a raid on British positions: possible targets at Alexandria, Port Said, the Suez Canal and Tel Aviv in Palestine.

008ww2/2 Two Italian soldiers of the Bersaglieri regiment at an ancient Turkish fort south of Derna. They are wearing the traditional black feathers of the crack regiment in their helmets.

The Western Desert Campaign began 13 September 1940 with the Italian invasion of Egypt. The goal of the Italian 10th Army in Libya was to seize the Suez Canal by advancing along the Egyptian coast. After many delays the offensive was reduced to an advance of sixty miles halting with the capture of Sidi Barrani. The Italians consolidated their gains by constructing fortified camps and began to accumulate supplies for a continued advance on Mersa Matruh, about eighty miles further east, which was the base of the British 7th Armoured Division and the 4th Indian Division. However, a British five-day raid, Operation Compass, in December 1940, led to the collapse of the Italian invaders. Some units of Mussolini's 10th Army in Egypt that were not destroyed were forced to withdraw. The British pursued the remnants to Sollum, Bardia, Tobruk, Derna, Mechili, Beda Fomm and El Agheila, on the Gulf of Sirte. Operation Compass was a success, with British losses at 1,900 men killed and wounded. They took 133,298 Italian and Libyan prisoners, capturing 420 tanks and over 845 guns.

The defeat of the invasion force caused Benito Mussolini to seek help from Adolf Hitler, who responded with a small German expeditionary force. The *Deutsches Afrikakorps*, (*DAK*), landed at Tripoli in January 1941. It was commanded by *Generalleutnant* Erwin Rommel and placed under Italian command; however, in the event, Italian dependency on Nazi Germany made the *DAK* the dominant partner.

004ww2/2 *Maresciallo* Rodolfo Graziani North African Commander-in-Chief and the Governor of Libya. He planned the invasion of Egypt.

005ww2/2 The original caption: *Italian troops move up; this photograph, which arrived via a neutral country, was taken on Mussolini's famous North African coast road. It shows lorry loads of Italian troops moving forward to the Egyptian frontier, where the stern test of battle awaits them.*

009ww2/2 *Generale* Italo Gariboldi, commander of the 10th Army.

On 13 September 1940, four divisions of the Italian 10th Army advanced into Egypt and halted. Defensive positions were prepared by the Italians in fortified camps around Sidi Barrani.

CRETE
Scarpanto
CYPRUS (BR.)

TRIPOLI
Homs
Misurata
Sirte
Agheila

BENGHAZI
Tolmetta
Tokra
Barce
Benina
Saluch
Cirene
Derna
Gazala
Tobruk
Bardia
Collum
Ft. Capuzzo
Halfaya
Sidi Barrani
Mersa Matruh

CYRENAICA

ALEXANDRIA
Port Said
SUEZ CANAL
CAIRO
Suez

I T A L I A N
L I B Y A

Jalo Oasis
Siwa

L i b y a n   D e s e r t

E G Y P T

100 50 0   100   200   300   400   500 MILES

007ww2/2 Fiat M11/39 medium tank rolling along the coast road into Egypt heading towards Sidi Barrani where the Italian 10th Army would dig in and wait for the British counter-attack. The tank's operational range was 125 miles, with a speed of 20 mph on roads. Its main armament was a 37 mm Vickers-Terni L/40 gun and it carried eighty-four rounds. The tank had a crew of three: commander/radio operator; loader/gunner; driver.

010ww2/2 An Italian mortar crew operating a Brixia Model 35 weapon. It was a rapid firing light mortar, mounted on a legged base and designed for operation by a two-man team. The rear legs were fitted with a pad for the gunner to lie forward on behind the mortar; or sit upon when the situation allowed. A well trained team could discharge up to eighteen rounds per minute.

Generale Annibale Bergonzoli, commanding **XXIII Corpo**.

Generale Carlo Spatocco, commanding **XXI Corpo**.

Generale Sebastiano Gallina, commanding **Gruppo Div Gallina**.

Generale Ferdinando Cona, commanding **XX Corpo**.

Generale Enrico Pitassi-Mannella, commanding *XXII Corpo*.

016ww2/2 Two companies of Bersaglieri motorcyclists went in with the attack, one company with *XXIII Corpo* and the other with the *1a Divisione Libica*.

017ww2/2 Fiat M11/39 medium tanks on the drive into Eyptian territory.

018ww2/2 Men of the Italian forward battalions, of *1a Divisione Libica* spearheading the offensive across the Libyan border towards the first objective, Sollum. Facing the Italians was the 3rd Battalion Coldstream Guards, who were forced to withdraw to prepared positions .

Italian infantry pith helmet badge; metal on cloth cockade of the national colours of green, white and red.

020ww2/2 North African Commander-in-Chief, Rodolfo Graziani, inspecting a 'Blackshirt' company in Africa. The official name for them was the Voluntary Militia for National Security (*Milizia Volontaria per la Sicurezza Nazionale*), MVSN. Each man swore an oath of allegiance to Mussolini.

024ww2/2 Rino Corso Fougier commanded the Regia Aeronautica (the Italian Air Force).

MVSN insignia; helmet stencil badge.

023ww2/2 Fiat G.50 *Freccia* (Arrow) Italy's first single-seat, all-metal monoplane that featured an enclosed cockpit and retractable undercarriage, pictured flying over Egypt.

022ww2/2 SM.79 bombers of *193. Squadriglia, Regia Aeronautica* over North Africa, 1940.

026ww2/2, 027ww2/2. Blackshirts attacking British positions at Sidi Barrani.

-28ww2/2 The desert Egyptian-Libyan border outpost of Sidi Barrani.

032ww2/2 The Fucile Mitragliatore Breda modello 30 was the standard light machine gun of the Royal Italian Army. Feed system: stripper clips of twenty rounds.

Italian infantry weapon, Carcano rifle model 1891.

Carcano model 1938 cavalry carbine (moschetto), with folding bayonet.

033ww2/2 The MAB 38 (Moschetto Automatico Beretta Modello 1938), or Model 38.

030ww2/2 Italian artillery piece, the Obice da 210/22 modello 35, a heavy howitzer, in place at Sidi Barrani and pointing eastwards towards the British positions. Calibre was 8.3 inches.

025ww2/2 Italian wireless post set up at Sidi Barrani following its capture from the British.

034ww2/2 An anti-aircraft position with a six-man crew operating a 20 mm Cannone-Mitragliera da 20/77, produced by the Scotti works. It fired 250 rpm with a twelve round tray for the ammunition.

035ww2/2 Men of the *Compagnie Auto-Avio-Sahariane* (Auto-Saharan, Companies), an Italian military unit which specialised in long range patrols of the Sahara Desert. The units operated from the late 1930s to the Italian surrender in 1943.

036ww2/2 A machine gun post on the North African coast set up to help repel any British attacks from the sea. The weapon is the Fiat–Revelli *Modello* 1914, a watercooled machine gun used in both world wars. The steel helmets, M33, was adopted in 1934 and replaced the French style Adrian helmet.

037ww2/2 The *Autoblinda* AB 41 was armed with a 20 mm Breda 35 autocannon and a coaxial 8 mm machine gun in a turret and another hull mounted rear-facing 8 mm machine gun.

039ww2/2 Italian soldiers watch the shelling of British positions across No Man's Land.

038ww2/2 Italian mechine gunners using their anti-aircraft gun in the ground fire mode.

040ww2/2 Lieutenant General Richard O'Connor discusses the coming counter-offensive against the invading Italians with the Commander-in-Chief Middle East, Sir Archibald Wavell. O'Connor (left), commander of the Western Desert Force, issued his orders for Operation Compass on 6 December 1940.

Wavell ordered the commander of British Troops Egypt, Lieutenant General Henry Maitland Wilson, to plan a limited operation to push the Italians back – **Operation Compass**.

Lieutenant General Henry Maitland Wilson, commanding **British Troops Egypt.**

The British plan: it was originally conceived as a five-day raid with the possibility of continuing the operation if successful. It would be led by British armour; the 7th Armoured Division and 4th Indian Division would drive through the Sofafi-Nibeiwa gap. An Indian brigade and Infantry tanks of 7th Royal Tank Regiment (7th RTR) would attack Nibeiwa from the west, as the 7th Armoured Division protected their northern flank. Once Nibeiwa was captured, a second Indian brigade and the 7th RTR would attack the fortified positions – Tummars. Selby Force (3rd Battalion Coldstream Guards plus some artillery) was to contain the enemy camp at Maktila on the coast; the Royal Navy would give supporting fire by bombarding Maktila and Sidi Barrani.

Major General Iven Mackay, commanding **6th Australian Division** *(Reinforcements from 12 December onwards.)*

The British attack: Throughout the night of 7/8 December aircraft bombed the Italian fortified camps, their engines masking the sound of the attackers. The assault began at 7.30 am, taking the Italians by surprise and twenty-eight tanks were destroyed. The Italian and Libyan garrison resisted with great determination but were systematically overrun by a combination of tanks, artillery firing from point-blank range and infantry. British tanks broke through defensive walls and drove into the Maletti Group fortified outpost, where the Italians had just breakfasted. At 7.45 am the British and Indian infantry followed up on board lorries, which stopped 700 yards away for the men to disembark and charge into the camp. The Italian and Libyan artillerymen found that even field artillery shells fired at thirty yards range bounced off the armour of the Matilda tanks. By 10.40 am the last Italian resistance was overcome. Large amounts of supplies and water were discovered intact.

Major General Michael O'Moore Creagh, commanding **7th Armoured Division.**

Major General Noel Beresford-Pierse, commanding **4th Indian Division.**

OPERATION COMPASS
The Battle of Sidi Barrani
8-10 December 1940

HMS Ladybird
HMS Terror
HMS Aphid

SIDI BARRANI
MAKTILA
Bir Qasim Mahmud
Bir Hiweishj
Alam el Dab
Pt 51
Azziziya
Selby Force
Mersa Matruh →
BUQ BUQ
16 Brigade Brit
Tummar Central
Ilwet Matrud
Tummar West
5 Brigade Ind
Pt 90 Tummar East
4 Armd Brigade
7 Armd Brigade
Maletti Group
NEBEIWA
11 Brigade Ind
4/7 Rajputs
Support Group
Bir Enba
Rabia
Sofafis
Escarpment

4 INDIAN DIVISION
7 ARMD DIVISION
Sanyet Aulad Ali

050ww2/2 Photographed during Operation Compass: the British Infantry Tank Mark II, the Matilda. Forty-eight of these slammed into the Italian fortified camp at Nibeiwa and routed the 2 Armoured Battalion.

052ww2/2 Italian 'soft-skinned' vehicles after being bombed and strafed by the RAF during the opening phase of Operation Compass.

053ww2/2, 054ww2/2. A field gun surrounded by its dead crew in the Italian camp at Nibeiwa, garrisoned by the *Raggruppamento Maletti (*Maletti Group). Indian troops had captured the first of the strongpoints; 500 prisoners had been taken and the commander, *Generale* Pietro Maletti, had been killed in the fighting (inset).

051ww2/2 British troops take a rest during the fighting around Sidi Barrani. They appear to be eating from cans of food.

056ww2/2 During the advance into Libya men of the 4th Indian Division come upon a burnt out Italian SM 79 bomber.

055ww2/2 Some of the forty-eight Italian tanks captured or destroyed at Nibeiwa. The surprise attack was such that few of the crews reached their tanks before the vehicles were knocked out.

058ww2/2 Italian prisoners marching through Sidi Barrani. In just three days, from 9 to 11 December, 38,000 prisoners were captured.

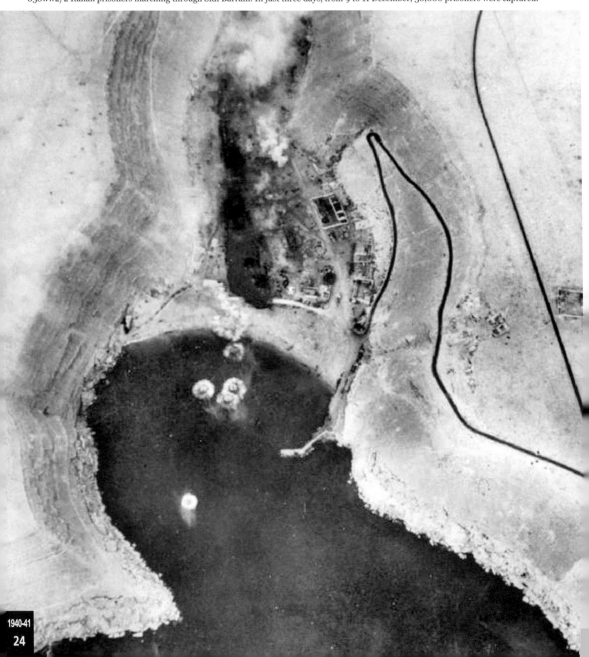

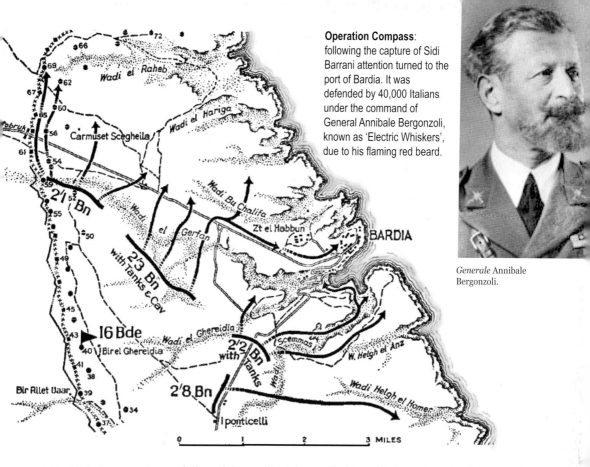

Generale Annibale Bergonzoli.

066ww2/2 Bardia being bombed by the Desert Air Force before the Australian attack.

In the early hours of the 3 January 1941 Australian troops formed up for an assault on the garrison of Bardia, the first town with a port in the line of advance along the coast. It was a bitterly cold night and men found the water freezing in their water bottles. A heavy artillery bombardment preceded the attack, supported by naval gunfire from the sea. Then the main infantry assault moved forward with Bangalore torpedoes to blow gaps in the Italian wire. The Italian defensive positions were soon breached. Resistance was mixed: some units surrendered immediately, while others put up a fight. As the day progressed increasing numbers of Italians sought to escape further along the coast towards Tobruk.

Major General Iven Mackay, commanding 6th Australian Division

065ww2/2 A 7.2-inch howitzer in action during the attack on Bardia, 31 December 1940.

067ww2/2 A 7.2-inch howitzer in action during the attack on Bardia, 31 December 1940.

069ww2/2 Australian infantrymen in a captured trench on the Bardia perimeter raise a grin for the camera before they attack again.

064ww2/2 Men of the Australian Division during the attack on the Italian defences at Bardia.

070ww2/2 Italian officers of an armoured unit at Bardia before the Australian attack.

071ww2/2 A Bersaglieri five man crew of a 47mm Cannone da 47/32 mod.35 anti-tank gun.

063ww2/2 The moment of surrender – Italians giving up as the battle for Bardia came to a close. Fighting spirit differed among the Italian troops; some put up fierce resistance whilst others were less than enthusiastic for the fight.

072ww2/2 Troops from the 2/2nd Infantry Battalion, Australian 6th Division, take the port of Bardia at bayonet point.

081ww2/2 A Roman Catholic priest says Mass for soldiers of that Faith following the military success at Bardia. They appear to be men of a Free French unit.

068ww2/2 The road above Bardia after its capture by the 6th Australian Division. A despatch rider checks out a couple of Italian L3 tankettes. Over one hundred of these light tanks were captured around Bardia. The sea port fell to the Allies on 5 January 1941 after a twenty day siege.

062ww2/2 When the Bardia area fell to the Australians over 38,000 Italians were captured. Included were four generals and large quantities of equipment. Here a column of prisoners stretches over the horizon marching eastwards towards Alexandria.

073ww2/2 Sixteen Italian M11/39 and M11/40 tankettes captured at Bardia were brought into working order and crewed by men of the 6th Australian Cavalry, carrier platoons. Large white Kangeroos were painted on them to avoid misidentification. They were used in the attack on Tobruk.

074ww2/2, 076ww2/2. Light tanks MkVIBs and carriers of the Australian forces driving on towards Tobruk. Infantry moving through a gap in the Tobruk perimeter wire. A barrage of seventy-five guns manned by Australian forces heralded the attack on 21 January 1941.

After taking Bardia the British drove sixty-five miles westward to the next Italian defensive position, Tobruk, a small port with a pre-war population of about 4000. Tobruk had a large harbour that could receive supplies to support a desert army. Australian forces, on 7 January, formed up on the Tobruk defence perimeter, which consisted of 128 defensive posts protected by an anti-tank ditch and barbed wire. The attack would begin at dawn. Royal Air Force bombers on nights prior to the attack carried out a number of raids.

On 21 January 1941, the day of the assault, naval gunfire from five ships shelled targets within the Italian perimeter. Supported by a British artillery barrage, the 6th Australian Division broke through the outer defences and fanned out. As the Australians moved towards Tobruk airfield and the town beyond, fierce opposition was encountered from machine guns, artillery and tanks. However, in the afternoon, Fort Solara, the location where General Petassi Manella, 22nd Corps commander, was captured. The next morning the commander of the Italian 61st Division surrendered. With the senior commanders captured and more than half the fortress in Australian hands, the remaining Italian garrison gave up. About 25,000 Italians were captured at Tobruk, as well as several hundred pieces of artillery, twenty-three medium tanks and another 200 vehicles. Australian casualties were forty-nine killed in action or died of wounds and 306 wounded.

075ww2/2 Tobruk with oil storage tanks ablaze, January 1940. The view is looking eastwards.

077ww2/2 The town of Derna was an Italian colonial settlement with a population of 12,000 before hostilities, but the settlers had evacuated the town in some haste. Both the natives and the Australian soldiers looted the dwellings before Major General Iven Mackay, commanding 6th Australian Division, restored order. The portrait of Mussolini, probably taken from one of the houses, is providing these Australians with some amusement.

In February 1941 El Agheila was taken by the British Western Desert Force following their destruction of the Italian Tenth Army and the Italian departure from Cyrenaica. Operation Compass had been a resounding success. The British halted at El Agheila while most of the Western Desert Force was moved across the Mediterranean to deal with the Mussolini's invasion of Greece.
It was time for Hitler to assist his fellow dictator.

078ww2/2 *Leutnantgeneral* Erwin Rommel paraded with his *Afrika Korps* in Tripoli 31 March 1941, prior to his deploying against Wavell in the Libyan desert. Considerable publicity was given to the event, which was arranged to demonstrate Axis cooperation, which Hitler saw as important in keeping the demoralized Italians on the right side.

080ww2 Hill 731: the toughest and most deadly battle of the Greek-Italian war, where the Italian Spring attack of March 1941 was halted.

Chapter Two: **Mussolini Targets Greece**

079ww2/2 Italian soldiers in the act of crossing the Albanian border and invading Greece on 28 October 1940. The Italians had to contend with the mountainous terrain on the border and fierce resistance by the Greek Army. In two weeks the invasion was stopped just inside Greek territory.

087ww2/2 HMS *Illustrious*, with Swordfish aircraft landing.

085ww2/2 Three battleships were hit by torpedoes, one was sunk and the two others seriously damaged.

Andrew Browne Cunningham, Admiral of the Fleet: *Taranto, and the night of 11–12 November 1940, should be remembered for ever as having shown once and for all that in the Fleet Air Arm the Navy has its most devastating weapon.*

British naval forces, under Admiral Andrew Cunningham, delivered a severe blow to Mussolini's pride when British naval forces attacked the base at Taranto, on mainland Italy, on the night of 11–12 November 1940. The Royal Navy launched the first all-aircraft ship-to-ship naval attack in history employing twenty-one obsolescent Fairey Swordfish biplane torpedo bombers from the aircraft carrier HMS *Illustrious*. The attack struck the battle fleet of the Regia Marina at anchor. The success of this attack augured the ascendancy of naval aviation over the big guns of battleships.

Mussolini's losses in North Africa had been an embarrassment to him and his expansionist ambitiions. Adding to his humiliation, his East African empire was scrubbed from the Italian list of possessions by a small force of British Colonial troops in a matter of months; giving the Allies their first strategic victory of the war. Italian forces had been pushed back from Kenya and Sudan, through Somaliland, Eritrea and Ethiopia.

089ww2/2 Colonel Orde Wingate, commander of Gideon Force, entering Addis Ababa.

084ww2/2 Prince Amedeo, Duke of Aosta, Commander in Chief of Italian military forces in Eritrea, Ethiopia and Italian Somaliland.

He made his final stand at Amba Alagi, a mountain stronghold on the Eritrean border. South African and Indian troops soon captured the surrounding lower peaks, turning the Duke's fortress into his prison. The duke and 5,000 men surrendered on 29 May, 1941. **Mussolini dismissed the defeat as having no effect on the outcome of the war.**

086ww2/2, 083ww2/2 South Africans at Moyale after the Italian forces had retreated. Emperor Haile Salassie returned with a small army in February 1940. He resumed his throne in Addis Ababa in May 1941.

082ww2/2 The dictator, Benito Mussolini, looks to territory he is determined to conquer – Greece. Il Duce had been annoyed when Hitler had invaded Norway, then Holland, Belgium and France without informing him first. *They behave as though we did not exist*, he declared to Marshal Badoglio, *I shall repay them in their own coin.* On 28 October 1940 he gave orders for a three-pronged advance into Greece.

090ww2/2 Italian soldiers during the attack on Greece, carrying a disassembled artillery piece.

091ww2/2 Italian infantry charging a Greek strongpoint during the invasion.

092ww2/2 On the Greek Albanian frontier an italian machine gun team moves closer to a jumping off position to give fire support to infantry and tanks.

094ww2/2 Italian Bersaglieri and L3-33 tankettes attacking Greek positions on the Albanian border.

098ww2/2, 099ww2/2
Mussolini's military leaders advised against a campaign in Greece during the winter months; weather conditions did not favour an invasion. However, the Italian dictator was not listening. Men of the 3rd Alpine Division *Julia*, after covering 45 kilometres of mountainous terrain in freezing rain.

096ww2/2, 097ww2/2. Greek gunners wearing the M1934/39 steel helmet purchased from Italy prior to the conflict as a replacement for their Great War Adrian helmets.

100ww2/2 Greek troops operating a three inch mortar. Italian invaders poured into Greece through the Pindos Mountains. This was difficult, terrain, made worse by the onset of winter. As Italian troops moved southward towards the city of Ioannina, Greek troops took to the heights, bombarding the Italians from above.

101ww2/2 *The Unsung Heroes of the Greek-Italian War* was one expression given to describe the support given by women folk. As the Greek soldiers in the mountains of Northern Epirus put up a fierce fight against the Italians, fully committed support was given by the Greek women in that area. In places where the army could not transport their equipment due to rough terrain they helped by carrying munitions, food and clothing.

The Italian ambassador visited Metaxas' residence and presented demands, which meant Greece surrendering sovereignty, on the night of 28 October 1940. Metaxas curtly replied in French: *Alors, c'est la guerre* (Then it is war). A few hours later, Italy invaded Greece from Albania and started the Greco-Italian War. Hitler was annoyed as he was focussing on his own invasion plans. The Greek Army was able to mount a successful defence and counteroffensive, forcing the Italians back and occupying large parts of southern Albania, called 'Northern Epirus' by the Greeks. Hitler would have to come to his Axis partner's aid.

102ww2/2 Ioannis Metaxas, Prime Minister of Greece from 1936 until his death in January 1941. On 28 October 1940, Ioannis Metaxas refused an ultimatum from the Italians to surrender Greece to the Axis powers. That stand by Metaxas brought Greece into the Second World War on the side of the Allies.

103ww2/2 Fascist dictator, Benito Mussolini demanded occupation rights to strategic Greek sites in his pursuit of war against the British. Also taking Greece would represent a further expansion of his new Roman Empire. The Duce had announced to his war council on 15 October 1940 that he would occupy Greece in a two-week campaign.

095ww2/2 An Italian casualty among the rocks in a gun position on an Albanian mountain side. Mussolini's invasion was a failure.

The Battle of Cape Matapan, 27 to 29 March 1941: this naval engagement was fought on the south-west coast of the Peloponnesian peninsula of Greece. Following the interception of Italian signals by the British Code and Cypher School at Bletchley Park, England, ships of the Royal Navy and Royal Australian Navy, under Admiral Cunningham, intercepted and sank or severely damaged several ships of the Italian *Regia Marina* under Admiral Angelo Iachino.

Vittorio Veneto

105ww2/2 Admiral Angelo Iachino, commander of the Regia Marina, the entire Italian battle fleet.

Defeat in Libya, setbacks in East Africa and humiliation in Greece prompted the Italian Supermarina (Italian Naval HQ) to attempt domination in the Mediterranean. Admiral Iachino was ordered to take a strong naval force and patrol the area north and south of Crete, sinking any British convoys or escort warships it might encounter. The Italian fleet was led by the new battleship *Vittorio Veneto*, screened by destroyers *Alpino*, *Bersagliere*, *Fuciliere*, and *Granatiere* of the 13th Flotilla. The fleet also included most of the Italian heavy cruiser force: *Zara*, *Fiume*, and *Pola*, accompanied by four destroyers; also the cruisers *Trieste*, *Trento*, and *Bolzano*, accompanied by three destroyers of the 12th Flotilla. Further, two light cruisers, *Duca degli Abruzzi* and *Giuseppe Garibaldi*, joined them with two destroyers. None of the Italian ships had radar.

HMS *Formidable*

HMS *Barham*

HMS *Barham*

HMS *Valiant*

107ww2/2 Admiral Sir Henry Pridham-Wippell, commanding Force B.

The British Mediterranean fleet, consisting of the aircraft carrier HMS *Formidable* and the battleships HMS *Barham*, *Valiant*, and *Warspite*, was covering British troop convoys to Greece, being carried out in support of the Greek forces fighting the Italian invasion threat. The main fleet was accompanied by the 10th Destroyer Flotilla (three destroyers) and the 14th Destroyer Flotilla (four destroyers); also present were two further destroyers: HMS *Hotspur* and *Havock*. Also available for action was the light cruiser squadron, Force B, under Admiral Sir Henry Pridham-Wippell, which consisted of HMS *Ajax*, *Gloucester*, and *Orion*, the Australian light cruiser HMAS *Perth*; supporting destroyers were HMS *Hasty*, *Hereward*, and *Ilex*. Allied destroyers assigned to convoy duty were also available: HMS *Defender*, *Jaguar*, *Juno*, *Decoy*, *Carlisle*, *Calcutta*, *Bonaventure* and HMAS *Vampire*.

The battle was a disaster for the Italians; they lost three heavy cruisers and two destroyers. Matapan was the military defeat that finished the Italian navy. The next time the Italian fleet came out in force was two years later, to surrender to Admiral Cunningham at Malta.

Originally, Adolf Hitler had been prepared to let the Italians wear the Greeks down and finish the war in the summer of 1941. However, in the light of Mussolini's string of setbacks he decided that likely British intervention in the conflict in Greece represented a threat to Germany. At a meeting of the two Axis leaders in October 1940 it was agreed that Germany would come to the aid of its Axis partner.

113ww2/2 Mussolini greets Hitler from the Munich train at the Brenner Pass, 4 October 1940.

The World's news agencies reported on the meeting and, in Britain, the press speculated around the Nazi news bulletin:

HITLER MEETS IL DUCE AGAIN
IN BRENNER PASS   London, Oct. 4

The talks lasted two hours and forty minutes. Afterwards the following communique, was issued:

Within the framework of a routine exchange of views, Il Duce and the Führer met for a cordial meeting, conducted in the spirit of the Axis. The leaders, in the presence of Ciano and Ribbentrop, studied all problems of interest to the two countries. General von Keitel was present during the last part of the conversation. The talks continued, during luncheon, at which the Foreign Ministers also were present. Agency reports say there is no doubt the talks mean a readjustment of the Axis Powers' plans and assert that a change has been made necessary to combat the unexpected resistance in the battle for Britain. It is considered that the prospects of a direct military offensive depend largely on the extent to which Hitler and Mussolini can agree on the possibilities of a successful attack on Egypt.

115ww2/2 The German Army reached Athens on 27 April and Greece's southern shore on 30 April, capturing 7,000 British, Australian and New Zealand personnel and ending the battle with a decisive victory. A Panzer Mk IV with her crew proudly pose for the camera.

Chapter Three: Hitler Targets Yugoslavia, Greece and Egypt

114ww2/2 British troops retreating to the port of Nafplio ahead of the German onslaught for evacuation to Crete. On 25 April around 10,200 Australian troops were evacuated from Nafplio and Megara. Two days later a further 2,000 men were evacuated from Nafplio.

126ww2/2 Prince Paul, Regent of Yugoslavia, during the minority of King Peter II.

128ww2/2 The old Court Palace, Belgrade, 1930s.

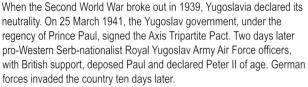

When the Second World War broke out in 1939, Yugoslavia declared its neutrality. On 25 March 1941, the Yugoslav government, under the regency of Prince Paul, signed the Axis Tripartite Pact. Two days later pro-Western Serb-nationalist Royal Yugoslav Army Air Force officers, with British support, deposed Paul and declared Peter II of age. German forces invaded the country ten days later.

129ww2/2 Minister of the Army and Navy, Milan Nedić, was replaced because he advocated that Yugoslavia join the Axis. After the invasion he collaborated with the Germans and served as Prime Minister of a puppet government in German occupied Serbia.

127ww2/2 King Peter II, aged seventeen, on 27 March 1941 was proclaimed King after a British-supported *coup d'état*. The bloodless coup was led by General Dušan Simović. When Yugoslavia collapsed, Peter fled Belgrade.

130ww2/2 Dušan Simović served as chief of the general staff and Prime Minister. Aviation was his main focus of interest. He joined other officers in a coup against the government of Dragiša Cvetković. After the coup, Simović became the new Prime Minister. He did not serve long in that role. On the wedding day of his daughter, 6 April 1941, Germany invaded Yugoslavia. Simović fled the country with his family.

131ww2/2 Dragiša Cvetković, the prime minister of the Kingdom of Yugoslavia from 1939 to 1941, signed the Yugoslav accession to the Tripartite Pact of the Axis on 25 March 1941. Two days later a group of officers carried out a military coup and Dragiša Cvetković was arrested, along with other pro Axis ministers. During the occupation by Germany he was arrested on two occasions. Finally he was taken to Banjica concentration camp. He escaped to Bulgaria in September 1944.

132ww2/2,133ww2/2. Original German caption reads: *Stuka attack on the fortress of Belgrade.* Outdated Yugoslav machines used for training set on fire by bombing on 6 April 1941. The small Yugoslav Air Force was wiped out in two days.

BULGARIA: after the failure of the Italian invasion of Greece, Hitler demanded that Bulgaria join the Tripartite Pact and permit German forces to pass through Bulgaria to attack Greece in order to help Italy. The Bulgarian government was reluctant to get involved in the war; but the threat of a German invasion, as well as the promise of Greek territories, led Bulgaria to sign the Tripartite Pact on 1 March 1941 and join the Axis

Bogdan Filov.
Prime Minister of Bulgaria

Ion Antonescu.
Prime Minister of Romania

ROMANIA: following the loss of territory to Soviet Russia, which had been gained in the wake of the Great War, the popularity of Romania's government plummeted. The Fascist and military factions, eventually staged a coup that turned the country into a dictatorship under Mareșal Ion Antonescu. The new regime firmly set the country on a course towards the Axis camp, officially joining the Axis powers on 23 November 1940.

From Bugaria, Romania, Hungary, Italy and Austria, the invaders swept into Yugoslavia, whose last minute revolution against the pro-Axis government of Prince Paul had interfered with Hitler's plans for further aggressive initiatives on the eastern frontiers of the Reich.

Operation Punishment, was the German bombing of Belgrade in retaliation for the *coup d'état* that overthrew the government that had signed the Tripartite Pact. The bombing occurred in the first days of the German-led Axis invasion of Yugoslavia.

134ww2/2 *Generalleutnant* Alexander Löhr, commander of *Luftflotte 4.* He was responsible for planning to bomb Belgrade with incendiary bombs first, so that the fires would help the second, night attack to find the targets. Among the non-military targets struck during the bombing were the National Library of Serbia, which burned to the ground with the loss of hundreds of thousands of books and manuscripts. This was the largest destruction of cultural artifacts in a single act in the Second World War.

136ww2/2 A street in Belgrade after the bombing. A sight that was becoming common throughout Europe.

138ww2/2 A Panzer division puts on a victory parade through the streets of an undamaged part of Belgrad

135ww2/2 Refugees seeking a safe place during the invasion of Yugoslavia pass a German Panzer Mk IV halted on the road to Belgrade.

137ww2/2 Some greet the invaders with the Nazi salute in Belgrade. It is likely a staged propaganda photograph.

139ww2/2 The English caption released with this photograph: *The* Oberkommando der Wehrmacht *announces: On the evening of 10 April, under the cheers of the population, German armoured troops arrived in Zagreb, the capital of Croatia. Pictured, motorcyclists of the 2nd Company, Reconnaissance Battalion, 14 Panzer Division, drive through an endless double line of euphoric citizens of Zagreb, who celebrate the arrival of liberators and the proclamation of the Independent State of Croatia.*

The invasion lasted about ten days, ending with the unconditional surrender of the Royal Yugoslav Army on 17 April 1941. Large numbers of the population refused to take up arms, instead welcoming the Germans as liberators from their government oppression.

140ww2/2 Adolf Hitler in Maribor, Yugoslavia. He ordered his officials to *make these lands German again.*

The terms of the capitulation were severe, as the Axis proceeded to dismember Yugoslavia:

Germany annexed northern Slovenia, while retaining direct occupation over the Serbian state and influence over the Independent State of Croatia.

Italy gained the remainder of Slovenia, Kosovo and much of the coastal Dalmatia region. It also gained control over the kingship in the Independent State of Croatia.

Hungary occupied Vojvodina in northern Serbia, and later annexed sections of Baranja, Bačka, Međimurje, and Prekmurje.

Bulgaria occupied Macedonia and some districts of eastern Serbia.

The German invasion of Greece began on 6 April 1941. The bulk of the Greek Army was on the border with Albania, from which the Italian troops had attacked in October 1940. German troops invaded from Bulgaria, creating a second front. Greece received a small reinforcement from British, Australian and New Zealand forces in anticipation of the German attack. The Greek army found itself outnumbered in its effort to defend against both Italian and German forces.

TWELFTH ARMY
Wilhelm List

9th ITALIAN Army
Alessandro Biroli

11th ITALIAN Army
Carlo Geloso

GREEK
FIRST ARMY

'W' FORCE
(Wilson)

SECOND ARMY
von Weichs

Surrenders
23 April

III Army Corps
Georgios Tsolakoglou

Leibstandarte SS AH
Josef 'Sepp' Dietrich

METAXAS LINE
ALIAKMON LINE
THE FRONT AT DATES SHOWN

MILES
KILOMETERS

British evacuation
routes

When the hopelessness of resistance became apparent, Greek General Tsolakoglou, along with other senior generals, surrendered to the commander of the *Leibstandarte SS Adolf Hitler*, SS-*Obergruppenführer* Sepp Dietrich.

'W' FORCE
Maitland Wilson

Lieutenant General Henry Maitland Wilson ('Jumbo' Wilson) was appointed to command an expeditionary force ('W' Force) of two infantry divisions and an armoured brigade to help Greece resist Italy and the subsequent German invasion in April 1941. The Allied forces were inadequate, but Churchill's War Cabinet had thought it important to provide support for the only country outside the British Empire that was resisting Hitler and Mussolini. Wilson completed the evacuation of British troops from Greece on 29 April 1941. The airborne invasion of Crete would follow.

145ww2/2 Lieutenant Colonel Alexiou Istratoglou, Greek Orthadox chaplain at Fleet HQ, Salamis Naval Base, carrying out devotional duties holding a religious icon for the men to worship. Original caption: *Young men from across the country rose up to defend their homes. They knew the fight was unequal. They were taking strength from their brave priests who were to be found at the forefront from the outset – the Church could not remain indifferent, it responded.*

148ww2/2 Italian armoured cars on the road in Greece. These vehicles are Fiat/Spa Autoblinda 41 types with a 20 mm autocannon.

160ww2/2, 154ww2/2 Some Greek citizens giving the Nazi salute to German tanks entering this town. A German officer asks directions from a Greek policeman, April 1941.

159ww2/2 Advancing into the heart of Greece along the main line from the frontier. These MkIII Pzkw are halted on the tracks. Note the bypassed Greek fortress on the hilltop.

158ww2/2 During the invasion of Greece the *2nd SS Panzer Division 'Das Reich'* (*2.panzerdivision SS*) making ordered progress along a mudied road. A mix of German equipment is evident in this photograph: Motorcycle combinations, (BMW R75); staff cars, open topped, AU/Horsch-Opel, a staff car used by high commanders in the field, the Horch EFm convertible and Dutch built Ford V3000 trucks (captured in 1940).

157ww2/2 Lightening advance by German troops gave another country a taste of the new Blitzkrieg method of waging war. Using a rough, yet novel, way of advancing, this unit was photographed on 16 April.

155ww2/2 Infantrymen from the Australian 2/2nd Battalion after crossing the Aliakmon River on ferries during their retreat from northern Greece following the German invasion of the country.

On 15 April 1941, General Wavell sent to General Wilson the following message: *We must of course continue to fight in close cooperation with the Greeks but from news here it looks as if early further withdrawal necessary.*

156ww2/2 A Ju 87B, Stuka, St.G.77 (*Sturzkampfflugzeug*) over Greece in April 1941. Markings for this campaign were yellow cowlings and rudders. StG.77 was operating from Prilep in Yugoslavia.

147ww2/2 View of the *Kilkis* under attack; the photograph was taken from a diving Ju87 Stuka divebomber. *Kilkis* attempted to get underway to evade the attacks, but she was hit by several bombs and sank in the harbor.

The hulk of the battleship *Lemnos* was bombed and sunk, along with her sister ship, *Kilkis*, at Salamis Naval Base by Junkers Ju 87 dive bombers, on 23 April 1941. The *Lemnos* had been disarmed in 1937 and used as a barracks ship. The two vessels were 13,000 ton Mississippi-class battleships originally built for the United States Navy in 1904–1908. As *Idaho*, she was purchased by the Greek Navy in 1914 and renamed *Lemnos*; her sister, the *Mississippi*, was renamed *Kilkis*. From the start of the conflict, *Kilkis* was used as a floating battery based in Salamis. Spare guns from both ships were employed as coastal batteries throughout Greece.

151ww2/2 General Georgios Tsolakoglou, commander of the Greek III Army Corps, arriving at the German HQ to discuss the surrender of the Greek army.

149ww2/2 Meeting of the German commanders to discuss the surrender of the Greek army. From left to right: SS-*Oberstgruppenführer* Josef (Sepp) Dietrich; *Generalleutnant* Hans von Greiffenberg and *Generalfeldmarschall* Wilhelm List,

153ww2/2 Greek prisoners of war, after the surrender of their leaders on the 23 April, 1941, making their own way to internment.

164ww2/2 Where the Italians under Mussolini had failed in their war on the Greek nation, the highly professional German military machine of Hitler swept all before them. The British Empire troops were on the run and being evacuated by the Royal Navy. Here a Germany infantryman operates the standard issue light machine gun, the MG 34, firing 900 rpm.

Operation Hannibal, 25 April 1941

The Corinth Canal, the deep cut dividing the North and South Peloponnese, with its single bridge, was assigned as a target by the Germans. Were they able to capture it intact, remove any demolition charges and then defend the crossing, it they would speed the advance of the German *XII Army* and cut off the retreat of British and Empire forces. German paratroops were to seize the bridge. The troops assigned to the task were commanded by *Oberst* Alfred Sturm and consisted of *52.Fallschirmpioniere* (parachute engineers) under *Leutnant* Hafner, supported by the 1st and 2nd battalions of the *Fallschirmjäger Regiment 2* (FJR 2), under respectively *Hauptmann* Kroh and *Hauptmann* Pietzonka. It would be a classic attack, with Kroh's battalion landing to the north of the bridge and Pietzonka's to the south. The engineers would then move to locate and remove any demolition charges on the bridge.

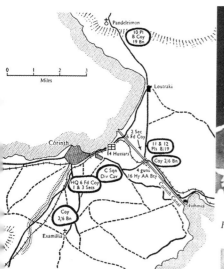

Disposition of British and Empire units defending the Corinth Canal Bridge.

Oberst Alfred Sturm, *Kommandeur Fallschirmjäger Regiment 2.*

Hauptmann Hans Kroh *1.battalion.*

Hauptmann Erich Pietzonka *2.battalion.*

170ww2/2, 171ww2/2, 172ww2/2, 173ww2/2. Early morning, 26 April, Ju 52 transports bringing in *Fallschirmjäger*. Jumping from aircraft, parachutes with containers and men landed on both sides of the canal, the bridge soon falling into German hands. Gliders with engineers were to follow.

162ww2/2, 174ww2/2, 163ww2/2. Operation Hannibal was going to plan so far: *Fallschirmjäger* in position around the captured road/rail bridge across the Corinth Canal; New Zealand troops being captured; German paratroops resting whi the engineers, who had arrived by glider, removed the demolitic charges from under th bridge. For some reason, however, the explosive charges, which had been removed from both sides of the bridge, we stacked on top, awaitir removal.

75ww2/2 Whoops! After the successful capture of the bridge, the demolition charges removed by the German engineers and stacked at both ends of the bridge were hit by a British anti aircraft shell. The combined road and rail bridge over the Corinth Canal was sent crashing into canal, blocking the way through for shipping.

76ww2/2 Isthmia, a small community at the south end of the Corinth Canal. The Germans built a pontoon bridge; their losses were light, only eight engineers were killed and a temporary structure was built across the canal by the morning of April 28. The capture of the Corinth Canal cut off the rearguard of the 4th New Zealand Brigade at Erithrae, but they were eventually evacuated from Port Raphti.

DT-SP7-14D
Kanal von Korinthos

Film Z 42/41 Bild 003 u. 004
St. St. Stuka 2
V. 26. 4. 41.
Bildzug mot. (Z)
712

Blatt 1:200000 Nr. 41/38

GR
M = etwa 1:8

177ww2/2 German aerial photograph, taken on the 26 April, the day after the attack. Four gliders that landed the German engineers are marked with the figure (2) showing the distance to the bridge marked (1), with two lines indicating the wreckage. Anti aircraft positions are marked (8).

180ww2/2 Messerschmitt Bf 110 fighter bombers from III.ZG 26 over Greece during the Spring campaign of 1941.

181ww2/2 On Sunday, 27 April 1941, the German Army occupied Athens; the German flag was hoisted over the Acropolis early that morning.

178ww2/2 Major General Bernard Freyberg VC, DSO** Commanding the 2nd New Zealand Division.

179ww2/2 New Zealand troops resting during their retreat before the German onslaught.

182ww2/2, 185ww2/2. On 21 April 1941, the decision to evacuate Empire forces to the Greek island of Crete and Egypt was taken. The Royal Navy evacuating Empire forces from Greece.

George II, King of the Hellenes. On 25 April 1941 the Greek ruler, King George II, along with his government, left the mainland for the island of Crete, which was attacked by Nazi airborne forces on 20 May 1941.

184ww2/2 British and Greek prisoners being taken to a temporary cage. The German Army reached the capital, Athens on 27 April and Greece's southern shore on 30 April, capturing 7,000 British, Australian and New Zealand personnel and ending the battle with a decisive victory.

The Führer and Supreme Commander
of the Armed Forces

Führer Headquarters,
25th April 1941.

Directive No. 28 'Undertaking Mercury' [Merkur]

1. As a base for air warfare against Great Britain in the Eastern Mediterranean we must prepare to occupy the island of Crete ('Undertaking Mercury'). For the purpose of planning, it will be assumed that the whole Greek mainland, including the Peloponnese, is in the hands of the Axis Powers.

2. Command of this operation is entrusted to Commander-in-Chief Air Force, who will employ for the purpose, primarily, the airborne forces and the air forces stationed in the Mediterranean area.

The Army, in co-operation with Commander-in-Chief Air Force, will make available in Greece suitable reinforcements for the airborne troops, including a mixed armoured detachment, which can be moved to Crete by sea.

The Navy will take steps to ensure sea communications, which must be secured as soon as the occupation of the island begins. For protection of these communications and, as far as is necessary, for the provision of troopships, Commander-in-Chief Navy will make the necessary arrangements with the Italian Navy.

All means will be employed to move the airborne troops and 22nd Division, which is under the command of Commander-in-Chief Air Force, to the assembly area which he will designate. The necessary space for freight lorries will be put at the disposal of the Chief of Armed Forces Transport by the High Commands of the Army and Air Force. These transport movements must not entail any delay in the mounting of 'Undertaking Barbarossa'.

For anti-aircraft protection in Greece and Crete, Commander-in-Chief Air Force may bring up anti-aircraft units of 12th Army. Commander-in-Chief Air Force and Commander-in-Chief Army will make the necessary arrangements for their relief and replacement.

After the occupation of the island, all or part of the airborne forces must be made ready for new tasks. Arrangements will therefore be made for their replacement by Army units.

In preparing coastal defences Commander-in-Chief Navy may if necessary draw upon guns captured by the Army.

I request Commanders-in-Chief to inform me of their plans and Commander-in-Chief Air Force to inform me when his preparations will be completed. The order for the execution of the operation will be given by me only.

signed: ADOLF HITLER

202ww2/2 *Generaloberst* Kurt Student. He planned Operation Mercury, the invasion of Crete.

188ww2/2, 190ww2/2. Men of the *5.Gebirgsdivision* (5th Mountain Division) preparing to board Ju 52 transports. They were to be employed in an airlanding role for Crete. Commander of the division: *Generalmajo*r Julius 'Papa' Ringel.

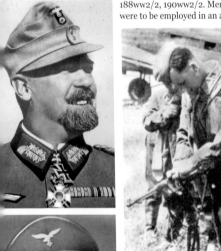

General der Flieger Freiherr Wolfram von Richthofen, *VIII. Fliegerkorps.*

192ww2/2 *Generalleutnant* Wilhelm Süssmann, commanding *7. Fliegerdivision*. During the airborne attack on Crete he was killed when the towline parted from the Ju 52, causing the DFS 230 glider, carrying him and his staff, to out of control and crash on the island of Aegina.

195ww2/2 *Fallschirmjager* check their weapons before their jump into Crete.
194ww2/2 An anti-aircraft unit loading their weapons at an airfield in Greece.

196ww2/2 Men of the *5.Gebirgsdivision* on a Ju 52 heading for Crete.

198ww2/2 *Fallschirmjäger* in a DFS 230 glider approaching Crete.

The Battle of Crete was the first occasion where German paratroops were used *en masse*: the first airborne invasion in military history; the first time the Allies made use of intelligence from decrypted messages from the Enigma machine; and the first time German troops encountered mass resistance from a civilian population. The three airfields of Maleme, Retimo and Heraklion were the targets for the German forces attacking Crete.

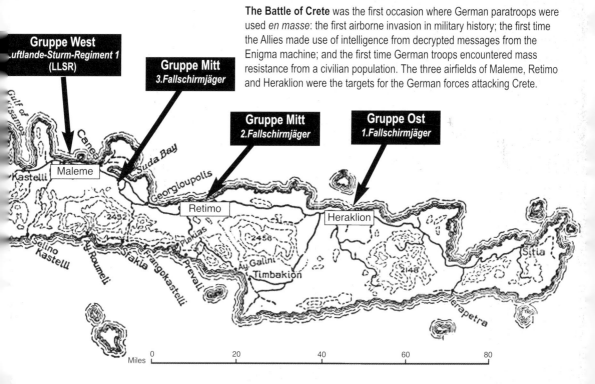

Gruppe West
Luftlande-Sturm-Regiment 1
(LLSR)

Gruppe Mitt
3.Fallschirmjäger

Gruppe Mitt
2.Fallschirmjäger

Gruppe Ost
1.Fallschirmjäger

9ww2/2 Junkers Ju 52 'Iron Annie' transports, some towing DFS 230 gliders, inbound for Crete.

211ww2/2, 152ww2/2. Allied troops await the invasion of Crete.

On 30 April 1941 Major General Bernard Freyberg VC was appointed commander of the Allied forces on Crete (Creforce). The Greek forces consisted of some 9,000 troops. The British contingent consisted of the original 14,000 British garrison on the island and another 25,000 British and Empire troops evacuated from mainland Greece.

212ww2/2 Major General Freyberg (right), Allied Commander at the Battle of Crete.

Brigadier Lindsay Merritt Inglis,
commander
4 Infantry Brigade

Major General Edward Puttick,
commander
2nd New Zealand Infantry Division

BrigadierJames Hargest,
commander
5 Infantry Brigade

225ww2/2 Gunners cleaning a 3.7-inch anti-aircraft gun in the Western Desert, 1941. The 151 (London Battery), 51st (London) Heavy Anti-Aircraft Regiment, was deployed with one troop at the naval base of Suda and the other at the airbase at Maleme. More than half the AA guns at Maleme airfield were knocked out by enemy action. On 26 May the Allied forces were ordered to retreat and the remaining guns were destroyed; some men escaped by boat. Many men became prisoners of war. 151 (London) Battery was so reduced that shortly after the survivors reached Egypt it was disbanded.

206ww2/2 Before the aerial assault the *Luftwaffe* attacked the anti-aircraft guns protecting the three airfields.

Opposite:
209ww2/2 The airborne invaders over Suda Bay.

208ww2/2 Few of the *Fallschirmjäger* were killed or wounded on their way down. However, because their weapons and ammunition were dropped in separate containers, recovering these under fire proved disastrous. Numbers of those not killed upon landing were put to death by civilians in horrific circumstances.

218ww2/2 One of many casualties among the olive groves. This man is still in his harness and with his chute caught in an olive tree, indicating that he may have been killed on the way down.

224ww2/2 An Australian Bofors gun crew on the hillside above the northern perimeter of Maleme airfield, May 1941. These are men of the 2/7th Battery, 2/3rd Light Anti-Aircraft Regiment. The 2/7th had sailed for Greece on 10 April 1941 with thirty-three officers and 726 other ranks. In Greece the battalion had lost seven killed and seventy-three became prisoners. From Crete, just sixteen men made it back to Alexandria.

Oberfeldwebel Helmut Wenzel:

Crete appears in the distance. Get ready! We stand and hook up the static lines of our parachutes. Check the harness of the man in front and prepare to jump. Clocking noise of bullets and little holes appear in the aircraft; this tells us that we are already under fire from the ground. Events reel off very rapidly as we approach the drop zone. The man behind me is hit and curls up on the floor, probably dead. There is no time to see to him – we have to jump! I jump ahead of my men, holding my camera with one hand, as it will not fit inside my jump smock – my gas mask is taking its place. As I float down, bullets whistle past me and I hear the crackling noise of small-arms fire. The enemy is giving us a hot reception and, looking down, I can see we are dropping right onto enemy positions.

213ww2/2 German paratroopers cut down and killed while gathering together following their landing.

214ww2/2, 215ww2/2 Having landed safely two paratroopers scan their surroundings to locate their comrades and enemy positions.

216ww2/2, 210ww2/2. Once reformed the *Fallschirmjäger* move off to engage and defeat the defenders of the Allied strongpoints.

207ww2/2 *Fallschirmjäger* searching a captured soldier of the 2nd Argyll and Sutherland Highlanders near Iraklio.

217ww2/2 A DFS 230 glider after a good landing on Crete; it appears to have suffered no flak damage. This is likely a post battle posed photograph.

20ww2/2 Some Empire troops captured during the fighting for a strongpoint in the hills.

219ww2/2 Tavronitas Bridge with a glider belonging to *Gruppe Brücke* ended up on the bridge approach banking. Of nine gliders detailed to land in the vicinity of the bridge, four ended up almost on top of it.

200ww2/2 *Generalmajor* Eugen Meindl, commanded *Luftlande Sturmregiment* during the Crete operation. He was severely wounded at Tavronitas Bridge.

229ww2/2 New Zealanders, during a lull in the battle, pose for a snap among the parachute draped olive trees.

203ww2/2, 204ww2/2. The massacre of Greek civilians at Kondomari, Crete, 1941. Twenty-three men were killed. It appears to have been carried out in a disorganized fashion: the victims have not been put against a wall and some can be seen running away from the bullets. This is not an orderly firing squad. The ones who fled would have had to be hunted down like animals, with all the resulting torment.

At Göring's instructions, General Student issued an order for the launching of reprisals against the local people; the massacre of Kondomari and the razing of the village of Kandanos were two notable examples. Student's orders:

It is certain that the civilian population, including women and boys, have taken part in the fighting, committing acts of sabotage, mutilation and the killing of wounded. It is therefore time to take action against all cases of this kind; to undertake reprisals and punitive operations, which must be carried through with exemplary terror. The harshest measures must be taken. I order the following: shooting for all cases of proven cruelty (I prefer this to be done by the same units who have suffered such atrocities). The following reprisals will be taken:
1. Shooting
2. Fines
3. Total destruction of villages by burning
4. Extermination of the male population of the territory in question.

My authority will be necessary for measures under 3 and 4. All these measures must be taken immediately omitting all formalities. In view of the circumstances of the crimes, the troops have a right to this and there is no need for military tribunals to judge these beasts and assassins.

26ww2/2 Two Cretan civilians bearing arms against the invaders. The Germans in both world wars took an uncompromising policy against irregular troops ranged against them. The difficulty in identifying an enemy who can easily melt back in among the populace after a belligerent act may be imagined. The German method in occupied territories was to take civilian hostages and execute them should there be hostile acts. Terror and fear was the way they combated the menace.

227ww2/2 A file of withdrawing Allied troops on the upper section of the route of descent through the Imbros Gorge to the south coast of the island, 30 May 1941. Some 9,000 surrendered to the pursuing Germans. About 18,600 men of the 32,000 British troops on the island were evacuated. Most were lifted from Sfakia on the south coast.

248ww2/2 A contributory factor to the high casualty rate among *fallschirmjäger* was the practice of dropping heavy weapons and ammunition in separate containers. On Crete these containers ha[...] be located, some fallen among olive groves, during the heat of ba[...] and the contents distributed to hard pressed paratroopers.

'Ich hatte einmal einen Kamerade.'
After the losses on Crete (5,894 casualties), Hitler considered airborne forces no longer enjoyed the element of surprise and therefore that advantage was lost. He decreed that the days of the airborne corps were over and directed that paratroopers were to be employed as ground-based infantry in subsequent operations.

231ww2/2 The Italian torpedo boat *Lupo*. During the German invasion of Crete in May 1941, while escorting twenty fishing boats, caiques, carrying 2,250 men of the *5.Gebirgsdivision* (mountain troops), it took on a superior force of British warships, three cruisers and four destroyers, in an attempt to save the troop laden vessels.

Italian captain, Francesco Mimbelli, chose to attack Force D, firing torpedoes and laying smoke to cover the escape of the twenty caiques packed with German soldiers he was escorting. The *Lupo* passed through the British force, avoiding collision with a cruiser, and escaped. Later, when the British had left, Mimbelli returned to pick up survivors from eight of the caiques. Six of the fishing vessels had managed to slip away. Only two vessels carrying reinforcements succeeded in reaching Crete.

Francesco Mimbelli, captain of the *Lupo*.

British Royal Navy, Force D
Rear Admiral Irvine G.Glennie.

Using information from Ultra code intercepts, the Royal Navy was able to intercept and disrupt the transportation of German troops by sea to Crete. The tiny Italian naval escorts, however, managed to save some of the vessels from the resulting carnage.

HMS *Dido* (37) Light cruiser – damaged.

HMS Orion (85) Light cruiser – damaged.

HMS Ajax (22) Light cruiser – damaged.

HMS Hasty (H24) Destroyer.

HMS Janus (F53) Destroyer.

HMS Hereward (H93) Destroyer. Sunk by air attack 29 May.

HMS Kimberley (G37) Destroyer.

The introduction of Rommel into North Africa.

Mussolini's ambitions in the Mediterranean had come seriously unstuck: his invasion of Greece from Italian occupied Albania had been a disaster. Hitler came to his Axis partner's rescue by invading Yugoslavia and Greece. Italian attempts to occupy Egypt and threaten the Suez Canal were repulsed. Worse still, the British, under Lieutenant General Richard O'Connor, had gone on the offensive and driven Mussolini's forces back towards Tripoli. Again, Hitler decided to come to the rescue. Italy must be kept in the war on the side of the Axis. It was decided by *Oberkommando der Wehrmacht* (the German Armed Forces High Command) to send a 'blocking force' of two German divisions to North Africa – Operation *Sonnenblume* (Sunflower). The commander appointed was one of Hitler's most capable generals, *Generaleutnant* Erwin Rommel.

Rommel was ordered to Berlin on 6 February 1941 to meet the Führer where he was told he would lead a new formation designated the *Deutsches Afrikakorps*. Hitler made it clear to him that, *The situation in the Mediterranean makes it necessary to provide assistance. Tripolitania must be held.*

Rommel arrived in North Africa on 12 February 1941, followed by the first German troops two days later. Rommel's first act was to fly towards the enemy positions so as to familiarize himself with the terrain over which he would be fighting. He immediately disagreed with the Italian commander, General Gariboldi, over the strategic course to follow. He was not for a 'blocking operation'. After conveying his views to Rome and Berlin, he prepared to go on the offensive against the British.

244ww2/2 Italo Gariboldi, Governor-General of Libya. In July 1941 he was relieved for his lack of cooperation with Rommel. General Ettore Bastico took his place.

'I believe it was a mistake not to have to have risked invading England in 1940. If this undertaking was ever to succeed, it would have been after the defeat of the BEF in France, when it lost most of its equipment. The longer invasion was left, the harder it would become for Germany to win.'
Rommel, March 1941

245ww2/2 General Ettore Bastico. On 19 July 1941, Bastico was named commander over all Axis forces in North Africa. As Rommel's superior in the North African campaign, his plans had to be first approved by Bastico.

247ww2/2 A PzKpfw Mk III being loaded on board a transport at Naples, bound for Tripoli. The tank belongs to *Panzer-Regiment 5*.

249ww2/2 Men of the newly formed *Deutsches Afrikakorps* marching across the Piazza Castello, Tripoli, being reviewed by the commander Rommel. 12 March 1941. They are wearing their new tropical uniforms, including large pith helmets.

246ww2/2 Marking the arrival of the *Deutsches Afrikakorps* in Africa a parade was held in the Tripoli. After speeches, in front of a statue of Mussolini, on the Piazza Castello, Rommel, his staff and Italian officers took the salute during a march past.

SIRTE

NOFILIA •

253ww2/2 Rommel in his command vehicle, a SdKfz 251/6 Ausf C half-track, during his opening moves in March 1941. He liked to be close to the action; within a short time he instilled a sense of elitism in the men under his command.

254ww2/2 The advance towards Egypt was on; an anti-aircraft unit in a Sdkfz 7 half-track towing an 8 mm flak gun. In the open desert fighting it proved deadly in the anti-tank role.

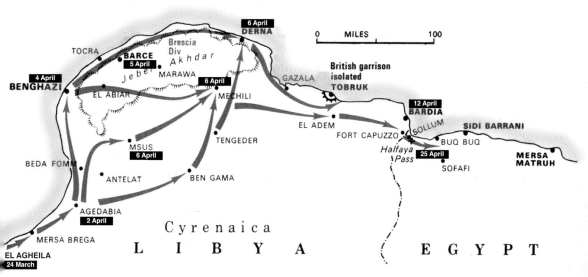

At *Generalmajor* **Erwin Rommel's orders** an Axis force rolled eastward and quickly defeated the British at El Agheila on 24 March and at Mersa el Brega a week later. A much weakened British force fell back into Cyrenaica. The Defence Committee in London had ordered that Cyrenaica was to be held with the minimum of forces and the surplus sent to Greece. The best-equipped units in Wavell's XIII Corps went to Greece. Rommel was quick to exploit the success and by 4 April, he had pushed the British back to Benghazi. The Italian Governor-General of Libya, Italo Gariboldi, was furious with his subordinate German ally for acting without direction. Rommel recorded:

Gariboldi was not at all pleased and berated me severly, mainly because our actions were in contravention of instructions from Rome. He demanded that I discontinue all such operations. I replied that I would continue to react to each situation appropriately as I judged at the time. The argument was brought to an end when the Oberkommando des Heeres [OKH High Command of the German Army] sent a timely message giving me a free hand to act as I saw fit. This brought our confrontation to an end in my favour.

The main factor in Rommel's success in taking Cyrenaica was Mechili, fifty miles inland from the coast. He directed three columns there and when it was captured on 6 April the British were forced to withdraw from Cyrenaica. Rommel had won his first desert victory.

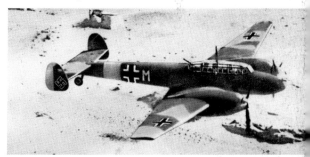

256ww2/2 Messerschmitt Bf 110Es of III./ZG 26 flew ground-strafing attacks to support German infantry.

255ww2/2 A SdKfz 251 half-track moving eastwards. This was the first place to be taken, El Agheila, The swastika flag draped over the bonnet is to identify it to friendly aircraft

257ww2/2 A Bersaglierie motorcyclist with a SdKfz 263 *Panzerfunkwagen* radio communication vehicle in the background. The Bersaglieri, with the distinctive cock capercaillie (wood grouse) feathers afixed to their hats, were an élite regiment of marksmen in the Italian Royal Army.

258ww2/2 Italian infantry advance past a PzKpfw MkIII during the attack on Mechili.

259ww2/2 A contributory factor to Rommel's success as a field commander was his practice of flying reconnaissance missions to survey up to date developments. Here he is returning from a sortie, doubtless with the latest information of enemy movements and the position of the forces under his command.

262ww2/2 A German 105 mm leFH 18 howitzer in action. It had a crew of six.

The Fieseler Fi 156 Storch (Stork). Rommel used the type for battlefield surveillance because of its short take-off and landing capability.

264ww2/2 Major-General Michael Gambier-Parry, commander of the 2nd Armoured Division. He was captured by the Italians along with Brigadier Vaughan, commander of the 3rd Indian Motor Brigade, at Mechili in April 1941.

263ww2/2 When Machili was captured over 3,000 men, British, Indians and Australians, were taken prisoner. Among them was Major General Michael Gambier-Parry, 2nd Armoured Division, and the officer commanding the 3rd Indian Motor Brigade, Brigadier Vaughan.

267ww2/2 Two captured senior British officers on the right, Major General Gambier-Parry; to his right, wearing sun glasses is Colonel Younghusband, his senior staff officer. Rommel has joined the group of his officers for this photograph (second from left with his back to the camera)

266ww2/2 A German platoon with four, three-man, machine gun teams, following up the advance of the motorized columns across Cyrenaica. Th belt-fed MG 34 had a high rate of fire – 900 rounds per minute – and was skilfully employed by the German soldier.

265ww2/2 Major General John Lavarack. With the capture of his generals, Wavell placed the Australian commander of the 7th Australian Division in temporary command of all forces in Cyrenaica.

261ww2/2 A British armoured command vehicle, of a type produced by Associated Equipment Company (AEC), was based on the Matador chasis. Three were captured and two were used by Rommel as mobile HQs. Both sides made extensive use of captured equipment.

269ww2/2 A knocked out British Light Tank Mk VIB on the Derna road. No doubt its adopted name would have caused many a comment and photo opportunity for passing Axis vehicle crews. The lorries on the road appear to be carrying fuel drums to replenish the panzer columns.

270ww2/2 Watching for the arrival of the Afrika Korps. A British outpost on the Tobruk perimeter.

268ww2/2 Captured British generals seem to be making the best of their predicament as they are about to climb aboard a Ju 52 for transportation to a prison camp in Italy. Left: Brigadier John Combe; rear, Lieutenant General Philip Neame; centre, Lieutenant General Sir Richard O'Connor; right, Major General Michael Gambier-Parry.

274ww2/2 The opening attack to break through the Tobruk perimeter began on 14 April 1941. These Wehrmacht officers are controling the fire of a battery of 105 mm howitzers from an artillery command vehicle. Map co-ordinates are being yelled to the crews through a magaphone.

271ww2/2 The Afrika Korps against the Tobruk perimeter: a PzKpfw IV Auf F and supporting infantry.

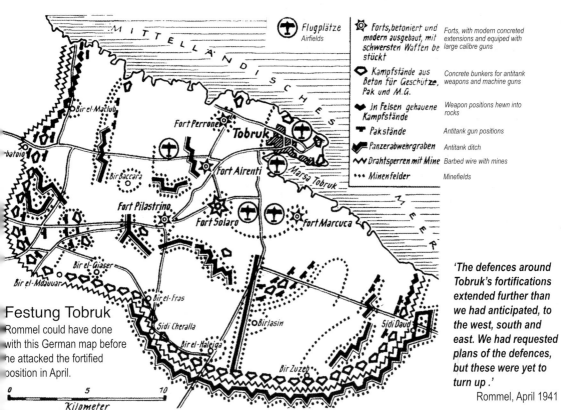

Festung Tobruk

Rommel could have done with this German map before he attacked the fortified position in April.

✈ *Flugplätze*	Airfields	
❋ *Forts, betoniert und modern ausgebaut, mit schwersten Waffen bestückt*	Forts, with modern concreted extensions and equiped with large calibre guns	
◆ *Kampfstände aus Beton für Geschütze, Pak und M.G.*	Concrete bunkers for antitank weapons and machine guns	
➹ *In Felsen gehauene Kampfstände*	Weapon positions hewn into rocks	
⊤ *Pakstände*	Antitank gun positions	
◤ *Panzerabwehrgraben*	Antitank ditch	
⌇ *Drahtsperren mit Mine*	Barbed wire with mines	
⋯ *Minenfelder*	Minefields	

0   5   10
Kilometer

'The defences around Tobruk's fortifications extended further than we had anticipated, to the west, south and east. We had requested plans of the defences, but these were yet to turn up .'

Rommel, April 1941

When Operation Sonnenblume (6 February – 25 May 1941), forced the Allies into a retreat to the Egyptian border, a garrison, consisting mostly of the 9th Australian Division, remained at Tobruk, to deny the port to the Axis, while the Western Desert Force prepared a counter-offensive. The Axis siege of Tobruk began on 14 April, when the port was attacked by the Afrika Korps and continued during two relief attempts, Operation Brevity (15–16 May) and Operation Battleaxe (15–17 June).

275ww2/2 A German gun crew firing their 105 mm howitzer at the defenders of Tobruk.

273ww2/2 Men of the Italian Divisione Brescia had been ordered by Rommel to draw the defenders to the west of Tobruk by raising dust clouds to make it look as though the attackers were preparing a major assault on the fortress from that direction. The truck is a light Cargo Fiat/Spa CL39, 'colonial' version.

276ww2/2 Australian troops occupy a front line position at Tobruk.

281ww2/2 A 25 pounder field gun with an Australian gun team in the Tobruk perimeter.

277ww2/2 General Sikorski visiting Polish soldiers in Tobruk.

279ww2/2 Major General Leslie Morshead, Australian defender of Tobruk and commander of the Australian 9th Division.

280ww2/2 Some of the first German army prisoners to be captured in Western Desert were taken in the fighting for Tobruk, 17 April 1941. An Aussie guard completes the picture.

282ww2/2 A knocked out PzKpfw Mk III during one of the attacks on Ras el Medauar, 2 May.

General Sir Archibald Wavell instructed Morshead to hold the fortress for eight weeks while the rest of Wavell's forces reorganised and mounted a relief mission. With the 9th Division, 18th Infantry Brigade and supporting forces from various Allied nations, Morshead's force defeated Rommel's powerful initial assaults and retained possession of Tobruk, not for eight weeks, but for eight months. An important part of Morshead's tactics was to conduct offensive operations against the beseigers. His attitude was summed up in a remark, made when his attention was drawn to a British propaganda article entitled 'Tobruk can take it!' Morshead commented: *we're not here to take it, we're here to give it.*
Use of snipers, artillery and counter-attacks were effective in keeping the Axis troops in a restless state of expectation. The Australian infantry dominated No Man's Land and made constant raids on enemy forward positions to take prisoners, to disrupt attack preparations and lay mines. The troops were backed up by well-sited artillery and mobile reserves. Axis propagandists described Morshead as 'Ali Baba Morshead and his 20,000 thieves', and branded the defenders of the port as the 'Rats of Tobruk'. It was taken as a compliment by the Aussies. They referred to Morshead humorously as 'Ming the Merciless', and later simply as 'Ming', after the villain in *Flash Gordon* comics

283ww2/2 Two Ju 87B diver bombers of *Sturzkampfgeschwader 2 (StG 2)* based at Derna in 1941 and engaged in attacking Allied shipping and Tobruk.

284ww2/2 Stuka dive bombers over Tobruk.

285ww2/2 Axis bombers and Stuka dive bombers pounded Tobruk throughout the summer of 1941. This Ju 87 burst into flames after being hit by anti-aircraft fire. It came down inside the Tobruk perimeter.

292ww2/2 Hans-Joachim Marseille. Top ace: all but seven of his 158 claimed victories were against the British Desert Air Force.

290ww2/2 Fighter pilots of *Jagdgeschwader 27* relax between sorties and pass the time playing cards and reading.

286ww2/2 A 3.7-inch heavy anti-aircraft gun team in action in the Western Desert, 1941.

88ww2/2 Ground crews watch the return of their charges: three Ju 87B dive bombers returning from a raid. he vehicle is a three door Kfz Stoewer 40.

89ww2/2 At Derna airfield a *Luftwaffe* officer briefs ground crews of *Zerstörergeschwader 26* against a ackdrop of their Messerschmitt Bf 110 fighter bombers.

287ww2/2 *General der Flieger* Hans Ferdinand Geisler, commanded the *X Fliegerkorps*.

294ww2/2 Air Commodore Raymond Collishaw, Air Officer Commanding, No. 204 Group (Egypt Group).

296ww2/2 Some of the first Hurricanes to arrive in the Middle East in November 1940 went to No. 274 Squadron, replacing its Gloster Gladiator biplanes.

293ww2/2 Groundcrew of No. 274 Squadron overhauling a Hawker Hurricane Mark I during the German siege of Tobruk. The squadron was operating from desert landing ground LG-010 at Gerawla, Egypt.

295ww2/2 Martin Maryland medium bombers of No. 39 Squadron operating from a landing ground in the Western Desert in 1941.

97ww2/2 Bristol Blenheim Mark IVs of No. 14 Squadron RAF over the Western Desert.

98ww2/2 A Martin Marauder of No. 14 Squadron RAF off the North African coast.

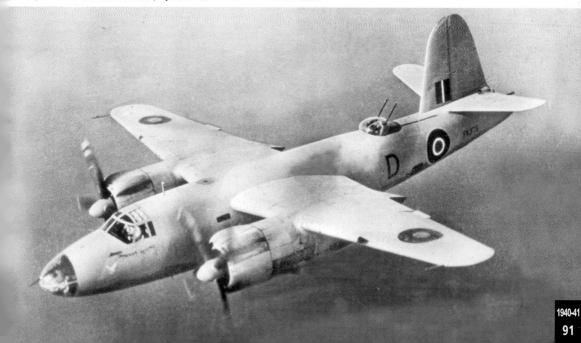

'The Armed Forces are infinitely stronger in every respect than they were a year ago, and we have every right to face the future with the utmost confidence.'

Winston Churchill
7 May 1941

Operation Battleaxe. On the 12 May 1941, a merchant convoy arrived at the port of Alexandria with tanks and fighter aircraft. Out of 295 new British tanks despatched 238 arrived safely. Just one transport ship, *Empire Song*, had failed to make it after hitting a mine. Forty-three crated Hurricanes had also arrived to reinforce the Desert Air Force. Churchill was insisting on an offensive to drive the Germans out of Cyrenaica and relieve the besieged Austrailians holding out at Tobruk. Wavell was expected to get on with the task as British air bases were needed between Sollum and Derna to counter the growing domination of the Germans in the eastern end of the Mediterranean following the occupation of Greece and the fall of Crete.

303ww2/2 Twenty-one light tanks, the Vickers Mk VIB, were landed in Egypt in time for Operation Battleaxe.

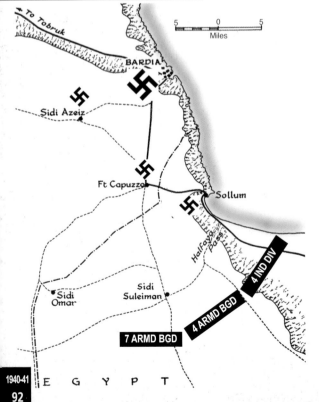

XIII Corps
Lieutenant General
Sir Noel Beresford-Peirse

7th Armoured Division
Major General
Michael O'Moore Creagh

4th Indian Divisio
Major General
Frank Messervy

4th Armoured Brigade
Brigadier
Alexander Gatehouse

11th Indian Brigad
Major General
Frank Messervy

7th Armoured Brigade
Brigadier
Hugh Russell

22nd Guards Briga
Brigadier
Ian Erskine

Support Group
Brigadier
John Campbell

278ww2/2 The Infantry Tank Mark II, better known as the Matilda in Egypt. Of the new delivery of armoured vehicles in May 1941, 135 were Matildas which went to the 4th and 7th Royal Tank Regiments.

301ww2/2 Eighty-two brand new Mark VI Crusaders, arrived at the port of Alexandria in time for the 'Battleaxe' operation to relief besieged Tobruk and drive the Afrika Korps and the Italians out of Cyrenaica. The Crusaders went to the 6th Royal Tank Regiment.

308ww2/2 Halfaya Pass, a 600 feet (180 m) high escarpment extending south eastwards from the Egyptian-Libyan border at the coast at Sollum.

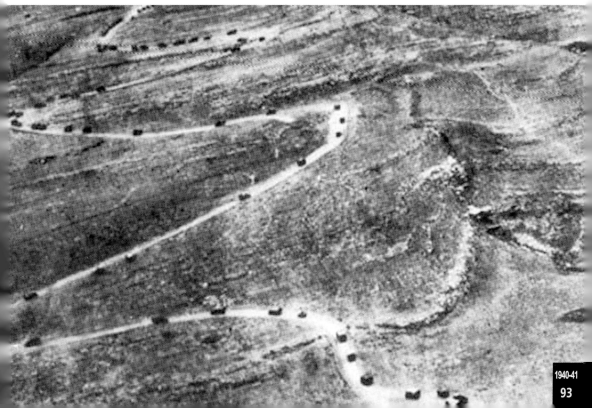

The Germans occupied the Halfaya Pass. Logistic problems caused the Germans to halt their advance into Egypt and they had dug in and fortified their positions at Halfaya with 88 millimetre guns. This was the anchor for the Axis positions, which opposed the Allied forces during their next attack — Operation Battleaxe on 15 June.

309ww2/2 Beginning of the gradient of the Halfaya Pass near the coast; 'soft-skinned' vehicles begin the climb.

310ww2/2 The crew of a dreaded 88 in action against British armour.

314ww2/2 No formation symbols on this Matilda, it could have been with either the 4th or the 7th Royal Tank Regiment. The British lost ninety-one tanks. The Germans lost fifty, but as they controlled the battlefield some of these could be recovered and repaired.

311ww2/2 Defender of Halfaya Pass, Hauptmann Wilhelm 'Pastor' Bach, (he was a Lutheren pastor) sited and operated his five 88 mm anti-tank guns with deadly skill.

252WW2/2 Rommel explains tactics to defeat the British offensive. He would report later: *'The crucial point in this battle was the Halfaya Pass itself, which Hauptmann Bach and his troops held throughout heavy fighting.'*

312ww2/2, 313ww2/2. Burnt-out Matilda tanks destroyed by 'Pastor' Bach's anti-tank guns.

315ww2/2 There were just five 88s in position on the Halfaya Pass front but they created havoc among the attacking British tanks. Another four 88s on Halfid Ridge and four more with Panzer Regiment 8 achieved similar results on their respective fronts.

'317ww2/2 Rommel confering with *Hauptmann* Bach, a colourful character in the Arifika Korps, Lutheran pastor and commander of 88 mm anti-tank guns defending the Halfaya Pass. On 29 June 1941 Rommel commented on their defeat of Operation Battleaxe: *The crucial point in this battle was the Halfaya Pass itself, which Hauptmann Bach and his troops held throughout heavy fighting. Also the Italian artillery battery performed with distinction in this engagement showing that Italian troops could give of their best when they had good officers. If the British had succeeded in taking the Halfaya Pass as planned, the situation would have been very different.*'

'The British seem very perturbed by our firm stand and probably wished they had not launched their last offensive.'
Erwin Rommel to his wife, July 1941

299ww2/2 With the failure of Operation Battleaxe Prime Minister, Winston Churchill, replaced General Sir Archibald Wavell as Commander-in-Chief Middle East on 22 June 1941. He made a straight swop with General Sir Claude Auchinleck Commander-in-Chief India. (left).

19ww2/2 The *Bismarck* was launched in February 1939. She, along with her sister ship *Tirpitz*, were the largest battleships built by Germany, and wo of the largest built by any European power.

Chapter Four: Hitler Suffers Annoying Minor Setbacks

8ww2/2 On 10 May 1941, the Deputy Führer of Germany, Rudolf Hess, on his own initiative, undertook a solo flight to Scotland, where he hoped arrange peace talks with the Duke of Hamilton as intermediary. Hitler was furious and directed the German press to declare him a madman. owever, it is now believed by some historians that Hitler may have been complicit in the peace venture of Rudolf Hess. The wreckage of Hess's esserschmitt Bf 110 in a field in South Lanarkshire, Scotland. Hess had baled out safely.

320ww2/2 The *Bismarck* left Hamburg for the first time on 15 September 1940.

324ww2/2 Hitler inspecting the *Bismarck*, 5 May 1941, with *Kapitän* Lindemann on his right and *Admiral* Lütjens alongside *Feldmarschall* Keitel behind. The vessel was now ready for her first operational voyage. Hitler discussed plans for a raid against convoys in the Atlantic.

Hitler expressed some concer that the numerical superiority the British fleet presented a great risk to the relatively sma German fleet. Admiral Lütjens was unconcerned about the British capital ships and prouc outlined the superiority of the *Bismarck* over any single Briti battleship. Her hitting and staying power were so great that he had no apprehension being outclassed. However, h voiced concern that breaking out to the high seas was a worry. Torpedo planes from British aircraft carriers were a great danger that he would ha to reckon with all the time he was in the Atlantic.

322ww2/2 Günther Lütjens (25 May 1889 – 27 May 1941). The German admiral was aboard the *Bismarck* when, on 27 May, he and most of the ship's crew lost their lives when the *Bismarck* was sunk.

In May 1941, Lütjens commanded a German task force, consisting of the battleship *Bismarck* and the heavy cruiser *Prinz Eugen*, during Operation Rheinübung. Lütjens was required to break out of their naval base in occupied Poland, sail via occupied Norway and attack merchant shipping in the Atlantic. The operation went awry when the task force was spotted and engaged near Iceland. In the ensuing Battle of the Denmark Strait, HMS *Hood* was sunk and three other British warships were forced to withdraw at speed. The two German ships separated. Three days later, on 27 May, Lütjens and most of the ship's crew lost their lives when *Bismarck* was caught and sunk in the Atlantic.

322ww2/2 *Kapitän* Ernst Lindemann commanded *Bismarck* during Operation Rheinübung. He went down with the *Bismarck*.

329ww2/2 Captain Ralph Kerr, captain of the *Hood*. He went down with his ship.

330ww2/2 Vice Admiral Lancelot Holland, commanded the British force in the Battle of the Denmark Strait in May 1941. He lost his life when HMS *Hood* was sunk.

333ww2/2 The German cruiser *Prinz Eugen* broke out into the Atlantic with the *Bismarck* in May 1941. The two ships destroyed the British battlecruiser *Hood* and damaged the battleship *Prince of Wales* in the Battle of the Denmark Strait. *Prinz Eugen* was detached from *Bismarck* during the operation to raid Allied merchant shipping,

327ww2/2 HMS *Hood* was hit early in the Battle of the Denmark Strait by several German shells and exploded. She sank within three minutes, with the loss of all but three of her crew: Ordinary Signalman Ted Briggs, Able Seaman Robert Tilburn and Midshipman William John Dundas.

332ww2/2 HMS *Prince of Wales* in 1941. Later that year, 10 December, she was sunk, along with HMS *Repulse*, by Japanese aircraft. On 22 May 1941, the *Prince of Wales,* the *Hood* and six destroyers were ordered to take station south of Iceland and intercept the German battleship *Bismarck* if she attempted to break out into the Atlantic.

328ww2/2 The final photograph taken of HMS *Hood*, taken from the deck of HMS *Prince of Wales*.

321ww2/2 *Bismarck* firing at HMS *Prince of Wales* on 24 May 1941 as seen from *Prinz Eugen*.

334ww2/2 HMS *Hood* with her forward guns turned to port. Photograph taken on another occasion.

335ww2/2 At a range of nine miles the sea battle commenced. The *Prinz Eugen* scored the first hits on *Hood*. This was followed by a fatal salvo from the *Bismarck* and HMS *Hood* blew apart. Only eight minutes after the engagement had begun this mighty ship had gone down with only three survivors. Lütjens turned his guns on the *Prince of Wales*. Within minutes shell splinters mowed down practically all her officers. Numbed by the defeat and himself wounded, Captain Leach gave the order to withdraw. The *Bismarck* is photographed firing the fatal salvo at the *Hood*.

326ww2/2 The column of smoke or flame that erupted from HMS *Hood* in the vicinity of the mainmast (immediately before a huge detonation obliterated the after part of the ship from view) is believed to have been the result of a cordite fire venting through the engine-room ventilators.

336ww2/2 Upon receiving news of the destruction of the Hood, Prime Minister Winston Churchill issued the order **'Sink the Bismarck!'**

337ww2/2 The Consolidated PBY Catalina, WQ-Z, piloted by Flying Officer Dennis Briggs and his American co-pilot, Ensign Leonard B. Smith of the United States Navy. (America was neutral, yet seventeen US pilots were flying with Coastal Command at that time.) The crew spotted the *Bismarck* and radioed its position. It was 26 May 1941.

340 ww2/2 Admiral John Cronyn Tovey orchestrated the pursuit and destruction of the *Bismarck*. He insisted on being a 'sea-going' admiral, despite pressure from above and the disadvantages of being away from command centres. When *Rodney* and *King George V* located *Bismarck*, they had the setting sun silhouetting them while *Bismarck* remained in the gloom. Tovey observed this and, to the surprise of his staff, ordered that action be delayed until morning.

343ww2/2 The *Bismarck* in the heavy seas of the north Atlantic. The Royal Navy was closing in.

HMS *Renown* and HMS *Ark Royal* operating at sea in Force H. viewed from HMS *Sheffield*. Following the sighting of the *Bismarck* by Catalina Z/209, Swordfish torpedo biplanes from HMS *Ark Royal* launched attacks on the German battleship.

41ww2/2 Part of H Force: aircraft carrier HMS *Ark Royal* flanked by the *Renown* and *Sheffield*. H Force had been despatched from Gibraltar with urgency, along with a screen of destroyers, to join the Home Fleet in a search of the north Atlantic. When the *Bismarck* was located HMS *Sheffield* shadowed her. The *Sheffield* was mistaken for the German battleship by aircraft from the *Ark Royal* and became the target for a torpedo attack (all missed or failed to explode).

On the 26 May HMS *Ark Royal* launched a strike force of fourteen Swordfish aircraft. Their orders were to proceed to the south and attack the *Bismarck* with torpedoes. Weather and cloud conditions were bad and a radar contact was obtained on a ship some twenty nautical miles from the estimated position of the enemy given to the leader shortly before takeoff. At 1550 hours they broke through the clouds and fired eleven torpedoes. Unfortunately the supposed enemy was HMS *Sheffield*, which managed to avoid all torpedoes. The *Bismarck* at that time was some fifteen nautical miles to the southward.

344ww2/2 HMS *Ark Royal* with some of her Swordfish aircraft.

347ww2/2 Fairey Swordfish biplanes ('Stringbags') from the *Ark Royal* made repeated torpedo attacks and succeeded in wrecking the steering mechanism of the *Bismarck*.

348ww2/2 Battleship HMS *King George V*, along with HMS *Rodney*, finished off the German battleship.

Thirteen torpedoes were launched by Swordfish from the *Ark Royal* and it was thought two hits and one probable had been obtained. The *Bismarck* had received a fatal blow and shadowing aircraft had seen her make two complete circles. One torpedo had struck on the port side amidships; another hit was on the starboard quarter, damaging her propellors, wrecking her steering gear and jamming her rudders. The *Bismarck* could no longer steer. The Germans hoped that while she was nearing the French coast aircraft and submarines would come to her assistance.

339ww2/2 HMS *Rodney* firing a broadside from her 16-inch guns.

345ww2/2, 346ww2/2. The battleship *Bismarck* on fire and surrounded by shell splashes. Viewed from one of the Royal Navy warships.

349ww2/2 Survivors from the *Bismarck* are pulled aboard HMS *Dorsetshire*, 27 May 1941. British warships rescued 111 survivors from *Bismarck* before being obliged to withdraw because of a U-boat sighting, leaving several hundred men to their fate. The following morning a U-boat and German weathership rescued five more survivors. Around 2,200 lost their lives.

Damage to the *Bismarck*

Survivors recounted the destruction:

The forward turrets seem to have been knocked out at 0902 hours. Then the forward control position was knocked out around 0912 hours. The after control position followed at about 0915 hours. The after turrets were at that time still in action. Then the aftermost gun turret was disabled by a direct hit on the left gun, which sent a flash through the turret. 'C' turret was the last one in action. At 0930 hours a shell penetrated the turbine room and another one entered a boiler room. By 1010 hours all secondary guns were silent. The upper deck was crowded with killed and wounded men who were washed overboard when the sea surged in.

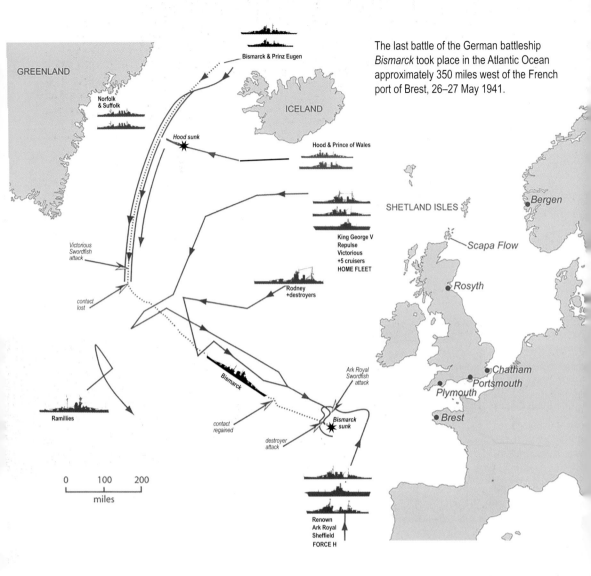

GREENLAND

Bismarck & Prinz Eugen

Norfolk & Suffolk

Hood sunk

ICELAND

Hood & Prince of Wales

The last battle of the German battleship *Bismarck* took place in the Atlantic Ocean approximately 350 miles west of the French port of Brest, 26–27 May 1941.

SHETLAND ISLES

Bergen

Victorious Swordfish attack

King George V
Repulse
Victorious
+5 cruisers
HOME FLEET

Scapa Flow

contact lost

Rodney +destroyers

Rosyth

Ark Royal Swordfish attack

Bismarck

Chatham
Portsmouth
Plymouth

Ramillies

contact regained

Bismarck sunk

Brest

destroyer attack

Renown
Ark Royal
Sheffield
FORCE H

0   100   200
miles

On 24 May the *Bismarck's* fuel tanks were damaged and several machinery compartments were flooded in the Battle of the Denmark Strait when HMS *Hood* was sunk. She intented to reach the port of Brest for repair. At one point *Bismarck* turned on her pursuers the *Prince of Wales* and the heavy cruisers *Norfolk* and *Suffolk* to cover the escape of the heavy cruiser *Prinz Eugen*. The following day the British ships lost contact with *Bismarck*. Later on 25 May Admiral Lütjens broke radio silence to send a coded message to Germany. This allowed the British to calculate the position of the *Bismarck* and aircraft were dispatched to hunt for her. She was rediscovered on the morning of 26 May by a Catalina flying boat from No. 209 Squadron and then shadowed by aircraft from Force H steaming north from Gibraltar.

The final action consisted of four main phases:
1. Air strikes by torpedo bombers from the carrier *Ark Royal*, disabling her steering gear and jamming her rudders, causing her to stay on a wide turning course.
2. Shadowing and harassment of *Bismarck* during the night of 26/27 May by British destroyers
3. The third phase on the morning of 27 May was an attack by the British battleships *King George V* and *Rodney* supported by cruisers. In under two hours of fighting *Bismarck* was sunk by the combined effects of shellfire and torpedo strikes.
4. Withdrawing British ships were attacked on 27 May by the Luftwaffe, resulting in the loss of the destroyer HMS *Mashona*.

On 10 May 1941, Hitler's Deputy Führer, Rudolf Hess undertook a solo flight to Scotland, where he hoped to arrange peace talks with the Duke of Hamilton, whom he believed to be prominent in the opposition to the British government.

351ww2/2 Rudolf Hess at the Führer's side during a march past.

353ww2/2 A Bf 110 of the type flown to Scotland by Hess.

Hess joined the Nazi party in 1920 and stood alongside his friend Adolf Hitler during the Beer Hall Putsch of November 1923. Following his arrest and trial, he served alongside his leader in Landsberg prison. There he took dictation for much of Hitler's book *Mein Kampf*. As deputy Fuhrer, Hess was positioned behind Hermann Göring in the Nazi hierarchal succession.

353ww2/2 Rudolf Hess after the flight to the Zugspitze (the highest mountain in Germany), in 1935 and landing on the upper Schleissheimer airport Oberwiesenfeld. He is welcomed by SA leader cronies and an unidentified woman.

354ww2/2 The wreckage of Hess's Messerschmitt Bf 110D in a field in South Lanarkshire, Scotland. Hess had baled out safely. He claimed he wanted to bring England to the conference table and make a peace settlement. Hitler was about to attack Soviet Russia and would have benefitted by a peace settlement with the British Empire.

The flight of Rudolf Hess flight was a remarkable effort: he managed to maintain his course for nearly 1,000 miles while consulting maps and his own handwritten charts. Furthermore, he managed to avoid interception by night fighters while flying over German airspace. He was picked up on radar by the British Chain Home station at Ottercops Moss near Newcastle upon Tyne and his presence was passed to the Filter Room at Bentley Priory. Soon he had been detected by several other stations, and the aircraft was designated as 'Raid 42'. Two Spitfires of No. 72 Squadron, No. 13 Group were sent to attempt an interception but failed to find the intruder. A third Spitfire sent from Acklington at 22:20 also failed to spot the aircraft; by then it was dark and Hess had dropped t a low altitude, so low that the volunteer on duty at the Royal Observer Corps (ROC) station at Chatton was able to correctly identify the aircraft type and reported its altitude as fifty feet. Tracked by other ROC posts, Hess continued his flight into Scotland at low altitude. However, he was unable to spot his destination, Dungavel House, so he headed for the west coast to orient himself and then turned back inland. At 22:35 a Boulton Paul Defiant sent from No. 141 Squadron based at Ayr began pursuit. Hess was nearly out of fuel, so he climbed to 6,000 feet and parachuted out. He injured his foot, either while exiting the aircraft or when he hit the ground. The aircraft crashed at 23:09, about twelve miles west of Dungavel House. He had planned to visit the Duke of Hamilton at

his home, Dungavel House, believing – mistakenly – that the Duke would be willing to negotiate peace with the Nazis on terms that would be acceptable to Hitler. Hess was transferred briefly to the Tower of London and then to Mytchett Place in Surrey, a fortifie mansion, designated 'Camp Z', where he stayed for the next thirteen months. Churchill issued orders that Hess was to be treated well. Three intelligence officers were statione on site and 150 soldiers were placed on guard. By early June, Hess was allowed to writ to his family. He also prepared a letter to the Duke of Hamilton, but it was never delivered, and his repeated requests for further meetings were turned down. Hess was moved to Maindiff Court Hospital on 26 June 1942, where he remained for the next thre years. He was allowed walks in the grounds and car trips into the surrounding countryside. He had access to newspapers and other reading materials; he wrote letter and journals. He became despondent when it became obvious that Germany was losin the war. Germany surrendered unconditionally on 8 May 1945. Hess, facing charges as war criminal, was ordered to appear before the International Military Tribunal and was transported to Nuremberg on 10 October 1945. He was sentenced to life imprisonment

355ww2/2 Hess in his cell, November 1945, at Landsberg Prison whilst awaiting trial. He committed suicide, still in jail, on 17 August 1987, aged 93.

69ww2/2 No sign of panic here as RAF personel take a break for tea and buns from a YMCA volunteer during an air raid on Dover.

Chapter Five: Hitler Targets Britain's Cities

68ww2/2 After the *Luftwaffe* had failed to win the skies over the south of England and had lost the Battle of Britain, it was ordered to target ports nd industrial cities. The Blitz became a night bombing campaign after October 1940.

571ww2/2 *Reichsmarschall* Hermann Göring with officers, France, October 1940. His prestige had suffered at the failure of the *Luftwaffe* to neutralize the Royal Air Force and it was decided to defeat Britain via strategic bombing. On 12 October 1940 Hitler cancelled Operation Sea Lion due to the onset of winter. By the end of the year it was clear that British morale was not being shaken by the Blitz, though the bombings continued through to May 1941.

By **September 1940** it had become obvious to Hitler that the *Luftwaffe* had failed to subdue the Royal Air Force and so win mastery in the skies over southern England. Plans for the invasion of the British Isles, code named *Unternehmen Seelöwe*, were revoked. Pressure through terror bombing and the cutting off of supplies across the Atlantic was to be stepped up against Britain, forcing Winston Churchill to sue for peace. In that month the *Luftwaffe* launched an eight-month campaign that would rain explosives on seventeen British cities and towns. The *Luftwaffe* gradually decreased daylight operations in favour of night attacks to evade interception by the RAF and the Blitz became a night bombing campaign after October 1940.

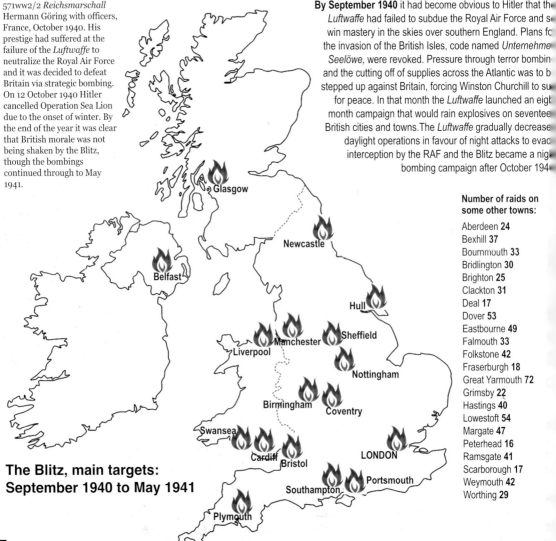

**The Blitz, main targets:
September 1940 to May 1941**

Glasgow

Newcastle

Belfast

Hull

Manchester · Sheffield
Liverpool

Nottingham

Birmingham
Coventry

Swansea

Cardiff · Bristol

LONDON

Portsmouth

Southampton

Plymouth

Number of raids on some other towns:

Aberdeen **24**
Bexhill **37**
Bournmouth **33**
Bridlington **30**
Brighton **25**
Clackton **31**
Deal **17**
Dover **53**
Eastbourne **49**
Falmouth **33**
Folkstone **42**
Fraserburgh **18**
Great Yarmouth **72**
Grimsby **22**
Hastings **40**
Lowestoft **54**
Margate **47**
Peterhead **16**
Ramsgate **41**
Scarborough **17**
Weymouth **42**
Worthing **29**

575ww2/2 *Generalfeldmarschall* Albert Kesselring commanded **Luftflotte 2** He targeted southeast England and the London area.

577ww2/2 *Generaloberst* Hans-Jürgen Stumpff commanded **Luftflotte 5** operating out of Norway against Scotland and Northern England.

574ww2/2 *Generalfeldmarschall* Hugo Sperrle commanded **Luftflotte 3** He targeted the West Country, the Midlands, and northwest England.

Operational orders [*abbr.*]:

    A = *Mondscheinsonate* (Coventry) [Moonlight Sonata]

    B = *Regenschirm* (Birmingham) [Umbrella]

Subject to appropriate weather conditions, it is intended to carry out two operations similar to the London ones, in which all units of *Luftflotten* 2 and 3 will take part. These operations will constitute large scale attacks against the English war industry. It is my expectation that during these operations the crews will maintain their previous keenly aggressive spirit.

It is a question of committing as many aircraft as possible. All other assignments are to be postponed on the day of the attack. Units being rested at the time are to take part.

588ww2/2 Because of heavy losses during daylight hours a switch to night operation was made in September 1940. Bomber crews being briefed at Venderville *Luftwaffe* base.

589ww2/2 *Oberst* Hans-Joachim Rath, commanded *Kampfgeschwader 4 'General Wever'*. He drafted the plans for the attacks on Coventry and Birmingham for November 1940.

591ww2/2 Mechanics and fitters working on engines of a He 111 of *Kampfgeschwader 4 'General Wever'*. Original caption: *Our aircraft must always be ready for the continuous retaliation of the Luftwaffe against England. The engine of a Heinkel He 111 bomber is being overhauled. A captured RAF crane proves useful for this work.*

Generalleutnant Walther Wever was killed in an air accident in 1936. At the time he was serving as Chief of Staff of the newly formed *Luftwaffe*. *Kampfgeschwader 4 'General Wever'* was named in his honour.

Kampfgeschwader 4

593ww2/2 Hermann Göring visiting *Kampfgeschwader 4 'General Wever'* Soesterberg airfield 16 October 1940, prior to the attacks on Coventry and Birmingham.

Coventry, Hitler's revenge: *Mondscheinsonate* [Moonlight sonata]

On 8 November 1940 Hitler attended the Nazi annual observance of the Munich Putsch of 1923, when he first made an unsuccessful bid for power in Germany. Sixteen of his fellow revolutionaries had been killed and he had been imprisoned. Each year a commemorative rally was held to honour the 'martyrs' of National Socialism and the Führer would deliver a speech. At the event the previous year, a German, Johann Georg Elser, had carried out an assassination attempt using a time bomb which killed eight people and injured sixty-two others. Hitler had left early before the bomb exploded. In November 1940 it was a particularly emotive occasion and on that day the RAF mounted a heavy raid on Munich in the hope of succeeding where Elser failed. Hitler was furious and hit back with the Coventry raid the following week.

The Courier-Mail
Brisbane 11 November 1940
RAF HAMMERS MUNICH
Hitler's First Taste of Bombi

One of the biggest fires was started by a raider which bombed from a low level, while in a shallow dive.

'Our target' said one pilot, 'was almost in the centre of the city. Before we left our base the intelligence officer who briefed us mentioned that it was the anniversary of the Beer Hall putsch of 1923 and that Hitler would be in Munich.'

594ww2/2
Servicing the
machine guns
of a He 111.

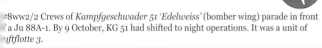

95ww2/2 Fuelling up a He 111E3.

78ww2/2 Crews of *Kampfgeschwader 51 'Edelweiss'* (bomber wing) parade in front
f a Ju 88A-1. By 9 October, KG 51 had shifted to night operations. It was a unit of
uftflotte 3.

582ww2/2 Two *Luftwafe* ground crew working on a Junkers Ju 88 of *Kampfgeschwader 54*, popularly known as *Schwarzer Mann* (Black Men) on account of their black overalls, October-November 1940.

580ww2/2 A German ground crew hauling bombs on a sledge to a He111 of *KG 54 'Totenkopf'* (Death's Head) in late 1940.

585ww2/2 Lifting a bomb in to the bomb of a Ju 88.

587ww2/2 Two 'black men' chalking up a joke message for the hated *Englische*. Perhaps alluding to the bomb being an eg gift for Easter (1941).

581ww2/2 using a mechanical lift to attach a SC250 bomb to a Bf 109E.

586ww2/2 A crew of a Ju 88 receiving assistance with their parachute harnesses. The external bomb load consists of two SC 250s and two SC 500s

576ww2/2 A Heinkel He-111H, KG 26, carrying a SC 1000 (*Sprengbombe Cylindrisch* 1000), a large general-purpose, thin cased, high explosive 2,200 lb bomb slung underneath, warms up its engines prior to take off.

598ww2/2 The pilot and navigator in the cockpit of a German Heinkel H-111 bomber. The navigator/bombaimer was usually the captain of the aircraft.

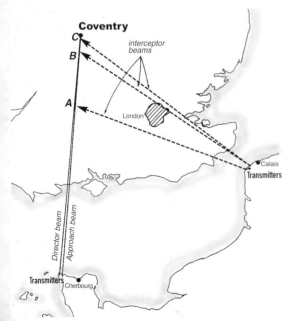

German *Knickebein** navigation system

Attacking bombers flew a course indicated by the Approach beam to the target city; three intercepting cross beams gave appropriate information and action to take:

First of the cross beams (**A**), code named *Rhein*, was transmitted from Cleve in Germany and alerted the aircraft crew that they were thirty miles from their target.

The second beam (**B**), code named *Oder*, transmitted from Julianadorp in the Netherlands, instructed the aircraft observer to press the button to start the bombing clock.

The distance to the target was now nine miles.

When the aircraft intercepted beam (**C**) *Elbe*, which originated from Bredstedt in northern Germany, the aircraft observer stopped the bombing clock; it was now just three miles to the target.

Shortly afterwards a timer made electrical contact and the bombs were released.

*Knickebein translates as 'crooked leg'.

596ww2/2 Observer {bomb aimer) on a Heink 111 at his bombsight. The steel helmet w standard issue to all bomber crev

600ww2/2, 601ww2/2, 602ww2/2. The air raid on Coventry on the night of 14 November 1940 was the most concentrated attack on a British city in the Second World War. The raid lasted eleven hours and involved nearly 500 bombers. The purpose was to destroy Coventry as a centre for war production. The *Luftwaffe* dropped 500 tons of high explosives, 30,000 incendiaries and fifty landmines. It was also trying out a new bomb – an exploding incendiary.

604ww2/2 The day after the attack, Saturday 16 November, 1940, King George VI visited Coventry and is seen here surveying the ruined medieval cathedral of St Michael's.

'All you could see was the searchlights. Occasionally, as they were swinging around, suddenly you might see a little silver dot and you would know it had picked up one of the planes. Then it would vanish. It was strange, seeing these little glimpses of the people who were bombing us.'

603ww2/2 Dazed citizens picking their way through the rubble after the attack.

606ww2/2 Just one German bomber out of the 450 involved in the raid was brought down. It crashed, killing its crew, thirty miles north of Coventry at Burton on the Wolds, still with its bomb load.

605ww2/2 Mass graves of the victims: 568 were killed and 863 seriously injured.

607ww2/2 John Bright Street, Birmingham, 20 November 1940. Firemen damping down fires after that night's *Luftwafe* attack.

Birmingham. Five days after the devastating attack on nearby Coventry a series of heavy air raids on the city of Birmingham took place. From 19 November 1940 to the 28th upwards of 800 people were killed and over 2,300 injured. Twenty thousand inhabitants of the city and surrounds had their homes destroyed. The first major air raid was launched against Birmingham, when around 440 bombers attacked the city, killing 450 people and badly injuring 540. A number of factories were badly damaged in the raid, including the Lucas Industries and GEC works. The Birmingham Small Arms Company (BSA) factory was badly damaged, causing loss of production and trapping hundreds of workers. Fifty-three employees were killed, eighty-nine were injured, thirty of them seriously and rifle production was stopped for three months. A member of the Home Guard and one of the company's electricians were later awarded the George Medal for bravery in helping the trapped workers.

Sixty bombers attacked Birmingham on 4 December and again on the 11th, involving 278 bombers. It was the longest raid of the Blitz, lasting for thirteen hours. Further heavy raids followed in March and April 1941. On the night of 16 May, another large raid caused damage to the Wolseley Motors factory and the ICI factory. However, after May, Hitler's attention was fully focused on the Soviet Union. It was the Russian people who would now feel the full weight of the Göring's *Luftwaffe*.

On the night of the 19 November 1940 a German bomber scored a direct hit on the Armoury Road site of the BSA factory at Small Heath. Many night shift workers had stayed at their machines when the sirens sounded. When they did decide to evacuate the factory the intensity of the raid made it difficult for them to reach the air raid shelters safely. They opted instead to shelter in the factory basement. Fifty-three were crushed to death when the factory building collapsed on top of them. One worker was rescued after being trapped for nine hours.

Important industrial targets – Birmingham

Name	Location	War Production
Aerodrome Factory	Castle Bromwich	1,200+ Spitfires & Lancasters
Austin Shadow Factory	Longbridge	2,866 Fairey Battles; Hurricanes; Stirlings and Lancasters
Austin Works	Longbridge	500 Military Vehicles/week
Rover	Solihull	Bristol Hercules Engines
Fisher and Ludlow	Birmingham	Lancaster Wings; Shell Casings; Bombs
Reynold	Birmingham	Spitfire Wing Spars; Light Alloy Tubing
GEC	Birmingham	Plastic Components
SU Carburettors	Birmingham	Aero-carburettors
BSA Factory	Birmingham	Rifles; Sten guns (100% of all made)

610ww2/2 A navigator in the nose of a Heinkel 111, approaching England's coastline.

Liverpool was of significant importance to the British war effort and, outside London, the most heavily bombed area of the country. It had, along with Birkenhead, the largest port on the west coast. The British government hoped to hide from the Germans just how much damage had been inflicted upon the docks, so reports on the bombing were kept low-key. Around 4,000 people were killed in the Merseyside area Blitz.

614ww2/2 Original caption: *The observer has a particularly onerous task of great responsibility during a night raid. He finds his way by the aid of a course calculator and a map, now and again using a torch to illuminate it.*

The George Cross and The George Medal

616ww2/2 Liverpool and Birkenhead area suffered two heavy raids on the nights of 20 and 21 December 1940. Over two hundred people lost their lives.

The George Medal and George Cross were decorations instituted in September 1940 by King George VI. They were to recognize brave acts during the Blitz carried out by civilians, both men and women.

13 March 1941.
A parachute mine fell on tenements in Adlington Street. **Sergeant Claydon** attended and organised the search and rescue work and the digging of a tunnel.

Bombs demolished houses and several people were trapped. Sergeant Claydon tunnelled twenty feet through the debris and rescued two women. He then shored up the tunnel with wood and masonry and, after strenuous efforts, succeeded in releasing another woman who was buried beneath rubble. The sergeant, owing to his exertions in a gas-laden atmosphere, was overcome and had to rest. He recovered and, though warned of the danger from gas, returned to the tunnel and continued his rescue work. A large piece of wood was wedged blocking the passage. Claydon obtained a saw, crawled into the space again, and, lying on his stomach, sawed through the block of wood and was able to release two casualties. Removing more debris he freed a child and a man and cleared a space so that others could effect the rescue of those remaining. Claydon showed exceptional courage in extremely dangerous circumstances and by his efforts ten persons were rescued.

612ww2/2 Police Sergeant Harold Frederick Claydon, Liverpool Police Force. **George Medal.**

...1ww2/2 Police Constable Edward Crann, ...verpool Police Force. **George Medal.**

30 May 1941:
Edward Crann was on duty when several bombs caused fires in buildings in the area. After displaying tireless bravery and saving the lives of four men, he was reported to have said: *There was nothing in it. I am no stranger to bombs, because, after being wounded at Ypres in the last war, I was blown out of a hospital bed by a bomb.* Prior to receiving the GM, Crann had been awarded the Police Medal for twenty years' service.

Citation: *During an air raid Constable Crann extinguished fires at a warehouse and an office, and was assisting the AFS [Auxiliary Fire Service] at another fire when a high explosive bomb dropped on the building. This caused the whole of the premises to collapse and become a raging inferno. The Constable, although severely shaken by the blast, searched for and found two injured and unconscious AFS men. With assistance the Constable carried them to a nearby air-raid shelter. Although there was grave danger from burning timber and collapsing walls, Crann returned and at once set to work to release a man who was buried. Being without tools of any description he removed the debris with his hands and after a time was able to extricate the victim and carry him to safety. The Constable then again returned to the burning building and rescued an injured and unconscious fireman. The Constable's unselfish and brave efforts, which were carried out in the worst possible conditions, were primarily responsible for the rescue of four men who would otherwise have lost their lives.'*

June 1941
James Wheeler was a part-time air raid precautions (ARP) warden in Liverpool. His act of great bravery took place during a raid on the city. Later, he gave a modest account of his actions, saying he wanted no credit. Police Sergeant Littledale assisted by holding a prop to prevent further debris falling.

High explosive bombs demolished houses and a woman and child were trapped. Mr. Wheeler began to remove debris whilst a prop was held under a wall to prevent it falling. The wreckage of the adjoining house was on fire and there was a serious escape of gas. Wheeler worked his way into a recess formed by the roof rafters. Any false movement would have been disastrous, for the rafters and the wall would have fallen on him. Smoke was pouring into the recess but, on his hands and knees, with a handkerchief over his mouth, he continued working for nearly an hour and rescued a woman and a little boy. Wheeler, on leaving the wreckage, collapsed but recovered and entered other badly damaged houses to continue rescue work.'

613ww2/2 James Henry Wheeler, ARP warden. **George Medal.**

1940-41

618ww2/2 Aircraft of the elite pathfinder unit, Heinkel 111Ps of *Kampfgruppe 100*. They were guided to their target with radio beams and used flares and incendiaries to illuminate the target for the main force. This was a system that was later copied by RAF Bomber Command successfully for raids on German cities.

The Sheffield Blitz occured over the nights of 12 December and 15 December 1940. The German code name for the operation was *Schmelztiegel* (Crucible).

On the first raid, 12th, thirteen Heinkel 111s from *Kampfgruppe 100*, the German pathfinder unit, arrived over the city at 7:40 pm and dropped sixteen SC50 high-explosive bombs; one thousand B1 E1 ZA incendiaries and 10,080 B1 E1 incendiaries. The main bomber force followed, numbering 280 aircraft made up of Dornier 17s, Heinkel 111s and Junker 88s For the second raid on the 15th, the Pathfinders used all incendiaries. Many steelworks received hits, including Hadfields, Brown Bayleys and Steel, Peech and Tozer Ltd. The damage was not serious enough to affect production. Six George Medals were awarded to citizens of Sheffield for acts of bravery during the raids. Over 660 people were killed, 1,500 injured and 40,000 made homeless. Three thousand homes were destroyed.

617ww2/2 Destruction in Sheffield City centre.

16ww2/2 Soldiers assisting with clearing up of the debris after the raid on Sheffield 12 December 1940.

20ww2/2 Two men of a Royal Engineers bomb disposal team working on an unexploded S.C.500 kg (1,000 lb) bomb in Sheffield.

621ww2/2 A landmine landed on this couple's back lawn and has been defused. The weapon was intended for use against shipping and had a high charge ratio of 60-70%, creating considerable blast damage in built-up areas. It had a parachute retarded descent and was designated *Bomben B* when used with effect against land targets.

Types of bombs used by the *Luftwaffe* in the Blitz:

50 kg	(112 lb)	**S.C.** or **S.D.**
250 kg	(550 lb)	**S.C.** or **S.D.**
500 kg	(1,000 lb)	**S.C.** or **S.D.**
1,000 kg	(2,400 lb)	**S.C.** (*Herman*)
1,088 kg	(2,400 lb)	**S.D.** (*Esau*)
1,400 kg	(3,200 lb)	**S.D.** (*Fritz*)
1,800 kg	(4,000 lb)	**S.C.** (*Satan*)

The weight ratio of the two most used types were **S.C.** 55% explosive, whilst the **S.D.** had 35%

S.C. stood for *Spreng Cylindrisch*, a thi cased, general purpose bomb. There was also the *Panzerdurchsclags Cylindrisch* **P.C.** which was a heavy armour piercing bomb used mainly against shipping and heavily shielded targets.

645ww2/2 Police and Army bomb disposal officers alongside a German 1,000 kg (*Herman*) parachute mine, just defused, Glasgow, 18 March 194

Leonard Harrison was the pioneer of bomb disposal and his findings from prewar experiments with fuses formed the basis for a manual followed by colleagues during the Blitz.

Pilot Officer Leonard Harrison, armaments instructor. **George Cross.**

Charles Henry George Howard, 20th Earl of Suffolk. **George Cross.**
He was appointed head of the Directorate of Scientific Research Experimental Unit. With his assistant, Frederick Hards, and his secretary, Eileen Morden, they became a tight knit team – known as the Holy Trinity. The team's primary work was to develop and try out ways of dealing with new types of unexploded bombs. They would work out ways to defeat the booby traps and other devices incorporated in them.

On 12 May 1941, the team took an old and rusted bomb that had been collected from a bomb dump in Erith, Kent and proceeded to examine it. The bomb exploded, killing Howard and his two assistants. He was awarded a posthumous George Cross and his two assistants the King's Commendation for Brave Conduct.

624ww2/2 Lieutenant Robert Davies of the London Bomb Disposal Unit looking for booby traps centered on the fuse of an unexploded bomb. Davies was credited with saving St. Paul's Cathedral from serious damage by defusing and removing another German bomb. **George Cross.**

642ww2/2 Firefighters attending the scene
of destroyed buildings at the Birmingham
Bull Ring, 9 and 10 April 1941.

William Mosedale, Station Officer and Rescue Officer, Birmingham Fire Brigade.

Citation:

An Auxiliary Fire Station was completely demolished by a very large high explosive bomb. A number of Auxiliary Firemen were trapped in the station and civilians were buried in an adjoining house that had also been demolished.

Station Officer Mosedale immediately began tunnelling and propping operations. Hundreds of tons of debris covered the site and Mosedale fully realised that at any moment he might be buried by a further collapse.

When the first tunnel was completed and the Control Room reached, he found that there were still men whom he could not extricate. He carried out another tunnelling operation from a different direction and again entered the Control Room. Five men were found, one dead, the others injured. The Station Officer crawled through and administered oxygen to the injured men and they were then taken out through the tunnel.

The entrance to the cellar of the private house was full of debris. Station Officer Mosedale directed operations for removing this, only to find that the cellar itself had collapsed. He nevertheless persevered and, after a time, reached seven people who were trapped. Three had been killed outright when the roof collapsed. He gave oxygen to the remaining four and succeeded in extricating them.

To reach other victims it was again necessary to tunnel, and Mosedale immediately commenced this work. The dangers to be faced were similar to those which he had found in reaching the Control Room. He nevertheless completed the tunnel and entered the cellar under the Fire Station. Four men who were alive were given oxygen and, despite their injuries, were safely removed. Tunnelling through such difficult material had necessarily been extremely hazardous, and the cellar collapsed completely shortly after the removal of the last victim.

These operations, which lasted more than twelve hours, were carried out under a most intense bombardment. Twelve lives were saved by Station Officer Mosedale, who showed outstanding gallantry and resource. In effecting the rescues he repeatedly risked his own life.

644ww2/2 William Radenhurst Mosedale, Birmingham Fire Brigade, was awarded the **George Cross** for the heroism he displayed on 12 December 1940 while working as a fireman during the Birmingham Blitz.

639ww2/2 A dramatic photograph illustrates the grave dangers faced by firemen during the Blitz.

652ww2/2 A fire started in Plymouth during a raid in November 194

653ww2/2 With the intense Blitz on Plymouth coming to an end, the Prime Minister visited on 2 May 1941 to thank the ARP, firemen, res and all the support and emergency services. The woman behind Churchill is Lady Nancy Astor, Lord Mayoress of Plymouth.

Plymouth in early 1941, in five raids, was largely reduced to rubble. By the end of the war, during the fifty-nine bombing attacks on the city, 1,172 civilians were killed and 4,448 injured.

On the evening of 22 April 1941, during an attack on the central area, the communal air-raid shelter at Portland Squar took a direct hit which killed seventy-six people (mostly by blast). Just three people in the shelter survived. During the Blitz the two main shopping centres and nearly every civic building were destroyed, along with twenty-six schools, eight cinemas and forty-one churches. In total, 3,754 houses were destroyed with a further 18,398 seriously damaged.

650ww2/2 Fighting the fires at Old Town Street. Eventually the wa supply ran dry and the fires were left to burn themselves out.

054ww2/2 A three-night blitz attack by the *Luftwaffe* on Swansea ensures a dramatic dawn after it ended.

Swansea's 'Three Nights' Blitz'.

Swansea's biggest raid, three nights' of intensive bombing, 19th, 20th and 21st February, lasted almost fourteen hours, Swansea town centre was completely obliterated by the 896 High Explosive bombs dropped by the *Luftwaffe*. A total of 230 deaths were reported and 397 injuries. Swansea was selected by the Germans as a legitimate target due to its importance as a port, docks and the oil refinery just beyond. The port's destruction was part of their strategic bombing campaign aimed at crippling coal exports and to demoralize civilians and emergency services (as in other British cities).

655ww2/2 Families in a working-class area of Swansea have tea and sandwiches from a mobile canteen after a night's bombing.

Manchester was hit by two nights of air raids in December 1940.
As a result of these raids, an estimated 684 people died and more than 2,000 were injured.

Manchester ARP Heavy Rescue Service located a family of four trapped in a basement. Two adults were extricated from an opening roughly 6ft deep and 2ft wide. Upon hearing that two children were still trapped under the debris, Alfred Ambrose Webster volunteered to attempt a rescue. He tied a rope to his legs and was lowered into the opening by men on the surface. After clawing his way through the debris with his hands, he located and rescued a child of twelve months. He went down a second time, with debris falling constantly, and rescued a second child of three years. As Webster and the child were hoisted to safety rubble and masonry collapsed, filling the hole in which Webster had just been working.

647ww2/2, 638ww2/2. Firefighters putting out a blaze in Manchester city centre after the German 'Christmas' raid, 22-23 December and again the following night, 23-24 December, 1940. One side of Manchester Piccadilly was almost completely destroyed in the raids.

548ww2/2 The dockside at Hull: A warehouse is still blazing fiercely as dawn breaks. Large-scale attacks took place on several nights in March 1941, resulting in some 200 deaths. However, the most concentrated attacks were between 3 and 9 May 1941, resulting in 400 deaths. Another large-scale attack took place in July with around 140 fatalities

A dramatic account of the raid appeared on Thursday, 8 May, 1941 signed: *'Anonymous'* – **In memory of the dead, the bombed out and those crippled in body and mind:**

Outdoors under a bright half moon, cable engines whine and balloons silently slip up to alert altitude. They are expecting visitors. Just after supper the sirens wail. Soon, a rumbling of anti-aircraft guns – way off. Windows rattle. Over my shoulder. Tiger the cat – ears pricking up – takes cover behind the great marble clock on the mantelpiece.

549ww2/2 Mulgrave Street, Hull, looking for survivors.

Out at the front of the house I stare between the gables over city and docks, the half moon is riding high under a fine May night. Way over the estuary, just discernible, are restless clusters of searchlights. The firefly stabbing of distant shell bursts. The grumbling of guns, increasing loud uneven throbbing now; heavy aircraft are approaching rapidly. The throb becomes a roar, filling the heavens. I am awestruck. Now the flares fall, row after row – I've never seen so many. Still more. The swaying chandelier-flares descend casting mobile shadows, illuminating the city in a milky-white light. It's almost as daylight. Now the local guns open fire, at first sporadically. As the flares fade a new glow bathes the skies, spreading and intensifying; this time the dazzling white glare from thousands of incendiary bombs rises from ground to the heavens. Transfixed, I watch the white glow turning orange and red. A hiss of bombs and I duck inside. Dad remains on the doorstep. It's only the sound of incendiary bombs – over our streets now. Above the glow searchlights playing on darker skies show up high-flying balloons and the smoke trails of snarling unseen bombers as they make their shallow dive-bombing runs. I dodge into a shelter with the others. The shelter gives a heave. Tentatively we look outside, but it's only windows gone, curtains streaming in the breeze, a downfall of soot. We are lucky. A fantasia of smoke trails in the searchlights, the shattering anti-aircraft gun cacophony, the deadly raittle of hot shrapnel clattering on tiles.

Hull is burning, but not beaten.

Rip the Blitz Rescue Dog

Over one hundred lives were saved by a mongrel named Rip over a twelve month period 1940 to 1941, during the London Blitz. The dog also located many bodies beneath the debris of fallen buildings, thus averting the threat of disease. The little East End stray was adopted by Mr E King, a warden based at Southill Street, near Poplar's Langdon Park. The little dog's keen sense of smell, and terrier-like instinct meant the mongrel was invaluable when it came to searching the rubble. Rip braved smoke, fire, explosions from delayed-action fuses, falling masonry and the inevitable danger of clambering over unstable debris; he seemed to know and act instinctively. When the value of search and rescue dogs were later officially recognized they had to be trained to do what Rip knew intuitively.

In 1945 Rip was awarded a Dickin Medal (often referred to as the animal Victoria Cross). He continued to wear the medal while engaged in his life saving work. Sadly, exhausted by the effort, he died in 1946. In 2009 Rip's medal was sold at auction for £24,250.

64oww2/2 Mr King working along with Rip to locate another victim of Göring's *Luftwaffe*.

36ww2/2, 633. Types of air raid shelters throughout Britain: street communal shelters were hastely constructed in many towns and cities. These [p]roved unpopular and even dangerous should a near miss destroy a wall, causing the concrete roof to come down. Anderson shelters were issued [fr]ee to all householders who earned less than £5 a week and consisted of galvanised corrugated steel panels. They were effective against bomb blast.

1940-41

646ww2/2 Tube stations and tunnels were vulnerable to a direct hit and several such incidents did occur: on 14 October 1940 a bomb penetrated the road and tunnel at Balham tube station, blew up the water mains and sewage pipes, and killed sixty-six people. At Bank Station a direct hit caused a crater of 120 ft by 100 ft on 11 January 1941, the road above the station collapsed and killed fifty-six occupants.

Dog - Owners

You are not allowed to take your dog into Public Air Raid Shelter-
but
BOTH YOU AND YOUR CANINE FRIEND ARE WELCOME HERE WHEN A WARNING IS GIVEN

NO RESPONSIBILITY CAN BE ACCEPTED

For Advice on any question affecting Dogs, ask
THE
NATIONAL CANINE DEFENCE LEAGUE
(a N.A.R.P.A.C. body)
VICTORIA STATION HOUSE, LONDON, S.W.1
(CHARLES R. JOHNS, Secretary)

635ww2/2 To increase the amount of shelter area for Londoners a short section of the Piccadilly Line, from Holborn to Aldwych, was closed to train traffic and converted for specific wartime use. This included a public air raid shelter at Aldwych. The lines are shown to be utilized as sleeping space (no live electrified line). Seventy-nine stations were fitted with bunks for 22,000 people, supplied with first aid facilities and equipped with chemical toilets. 124 canteens opened in all parts of the tube system. Shelter marshals were appointed, whose function it was to keep order, give first aid and assist in case the tunnels flooded.

HOW TO DEAL WITH INCENDIARY BOMBS

EQUIPMENT ~

TO SMOTHER BOMB WITH A SAND-MAT

TO DEAL WITH AN INCENDIARY BOMB

Never throw water on an incendiary bomb
it will explode ~

630ww2/2 A Boy Scount acts as a messenger between ARP posts – a bicycle mounted despatch rider.

A German incendiary bomb consisted of a cylindrical body, made of magnesium alloy, filled with thermite, an incendiary compound, to which was riveted a three-finned steel tail. These bombs did not explode; on impact, a needle struck a percussion cap, which ignited the thermite filling, and ultimately, the alloy casing itself. It produced heat sufficient to melt steel. They were thirteen and a half inches long, and two inches (5 cm) in diameter.

622ww2/2 From left to right: the 50 kg; the 250 kg; the 500 kg (in the wooden frame); the 1000 kg (nicknamed 'Hermann') and the 1800 kg (nicknamed by the Germans 'Satan').

643ww2/2 Flight Predictor operators at a 4.5 inch anti-aircraft gun site in Leeds, 20 March 1941. Note the enemy aircraft sillhouettes on the walls, one is of a Fiat B.R.20 *Cicogna* (Stork). Mussolini's *Regia Aeronautica* joined the *Luftwaffe* in bombing England; however they only operated over the south coast of England and to little effect.

627ww2/2 A 4.5 inch anti-aircraft gun in action against enemy raiders in the north of England.

8ww2/2 On the occasion of the sixth anniversary of the birth of the *Luftwaffe* its creator, Hermann Göring, discusses the bombing campaign
inst Britain with one of his pilots. The *Reichsmarschall* is embarrassed, having let his *Führer* down again. He had made loud claims that his
nted *Luftwafe* would deliver all that was required to bring about victory over the British: air supremacy over the skies of England and defeat of
RAF to ensure a successful invasion – that failed; bombing to devastation towns and cities so demoralizing the people that they would cause
rchill to sue for peace – that also failed to happen. It is 1 March, 1941 and the time for switching of the German Air Corps' efforts eastwards for
eration Barbarrosa, for preparation of the invasion of Soviet Russia is underway.

634ww2/2 London evacuees on their way to a safe place in the country away from Hitler's bombs.

During the period of the air assault on Britain, September 1940 to May 1941, approximately 190,000 high explosives and incendiar
bombs were dropped; 43,667 civilians were killed; 50,387 received serious injuries. Damage to property in Coventry by the end o
April 1941 amounted to 70,000 houses damaged. Prior to Liverpool's first big raid on 28 November 1940 the city had already bee
bombed fifty-seven times and 520 people had been killed. In the London area upwards of one and a quarter million houses had bee
damaged in the nine months of the Blitz.

58ww2/2 Soviet troops in Estonia 1941. Over 800,000 women served in the Soviet armed forces, although few were promoted to officer rank.

Chapter Six: **Hitler Targets Soviet Russia**

57ww2/2 Officers and NCOs of the highly successful German military machine scan Russian positions before attacking, June or early July 1941

The Führer and Supreme Commander of the Armed Forces   Directive No. 21
Führer Headquarters, 18 December 1940.   **'Case Barbarossa'**

The German Armed Forces must be prepared, even before the conclusion of the war against England, to crush Soviet Russia in a rapid campaign. The Army will have to employ all available formations to this end, with the reservation that occupied territories must be insured against surprise attacks. The Air Force will have to make available for this Eastern campaign supporting forces of such strength that the Army will be able to bring land operations to a speedy conclusion and that Eastern Germany will be as little damaged as possible by enemy air attack. This build-up of a focal point in the East will be limited only by the need to protect from air attack the whole combat and arsenal area which we control, and to ensure that attacks on England, and especially upon her imports, are not allowed to lapse. The main efforts of the Navy will continue to be directed against England.

I. General Intention
The Russian Army in Western Russia will be destroyed by daring operations led by deeply penetrating armoured spearheads. Russian forces still capable of giving battle will be prevented from withdrawing into the depths of Russia.

The enemy will then be energetically pursued and a line will be reached from which the Russian Air Force can no longer attack German territory. The final objective of the operation is to erect a barrier against Asiatic Russia on the general line Volga-Archangel. The last surviving industrial area of Russia in the Urals can then, if necessary be eliminated by the Air Force.

The effective operation of the Russian Air Force is to be prevented from the beginning of the attack by powerful blows.

II. Probable Allies and their Tasks
1. On the flanks of our operations we can count on the active support of Rumania and Finland in the war against Soviet Russia. The High Command will decide the manner in which the forces of these two countries will be brought under German command.
2. It will be the task of Rumania to support the attack of the German southern flank, at least at the outset, with its best troops; to hold down the enemy where German forces are not engaged; and to provide auxiliary services in the rear areas.
3. Finland will cover the advance of the Northern Group of German forces moving from Norway (detachments of Group XXI) and will operate in conjunction with them. Finland will also be responsible for eliminating Hangö.
4. It is possible that Swedish railways and roads may be available for the movement of the German Northern Group.

III. Conduct of Operations
A. Army (in accordance with plans submitted to me): In the theatre of operations, divided by the Pripet Marshes into a Southern and Northern sector, the main weight of attack will be delivered in the Northern area. Two Army Groups will be employed here.

The southerly of these two Army Groups (in the centre of the whole front) will have the task of advancing with powerful armoured formations from the area north of Warsaw, and routing the enemy forces in White Russia. This will make it possible for strong mobile forces to advance northwards and, in conjunction with the Northern Army Group operating out of East Prussia in the direction of Leningrad, to destroy the enemy forces in the Baltic area. Only after the fulfilment of this first essential task, which must include the occupation of Leningrad and Kronstadt, will the attack be continued to occupying Moscow.

Only a surprisingly rapid collapse of Russian resistance could justify the simultaneous pursuit of both objectives.

The most important task of Group XXI, even during these eastern operations, remains the protection of Norway. Any forces available after carrying out this task will be employed in the North (Mountain Corps), at first to protect the Petsamo area and its iron ore mines and the Arctic highway, then to advance with Finnish forces against the Murmansk railway. It will be the duty of the Finnish Army, in conjunction with the advance of the German North flank, to hold down the strongest possible Russian forces by an attack to the West, or on both sides of Lake Ladoga, and to occupy Hangö.

The Army Group operating South of the Pripet Marshes will also seek, in a concentric operation with strong forces on either flank, destroy all Russian forces west of the Dnieper in the Ukraine. The main attack will be carried out from the Lublin area in the general direction of Kiev, while forces in Rumania will carry out a wide enclosing movement across the lower Pruth.

When the battles north and south of the Pripet Marshes are ended the pursuit of the enemy will have the following aims:

In the South the early capture of the Donets Basin, important for war industry. In the North a quick advance to Moscow. Capture of this city would be a political and economic success and bring about the capture of the most important railway junctions.

B. Air Force. It will be the duty of the Air Force to paralyse and eliminate the effectiveness of the Russian Air Force. It will support the main operations of the Army, i.e. those of the central Army Group and of the vital flank of the Southern Army Group. Russian railways will be destroyed or captured at important points (river crossings) by employment of parachute and airborne troops.

C. Navy. It will be the duty of the Navy to protect our own coasts and to prevent break-out of enemy naval units from the Baltic. The Russian Baltic fleet will, with the capture of Leningrad, lose its last base and will then be in a hopeless position. After elimination of the Russian fleet the duty of the Navy will be to protect maritime traffic in the Baltic and transport of supplies by sea to the Northern flank (clearing of minefields).

I await submission of the plans of Commanders-in-Chief on the basis of this directive.

signed: ADOLF HITLER

The Eastern Front with the strengths of the German and Soviet forces prior to Hitler's offensive on 22 June 1941.

Feldmarschall Wilhelm von Leeb
ARMY GROUP NORTH

Feldmarschall Fedor von Bock
ARMY GROUP CENTRE

Feldmarschall Gerd von Rundstedt
ARMY GROUP SOUTH

North Front
(Popov)

L a t v i a
RIGA

EAST PRUSSIA   MEMEL

ARMY GROUP NORTH
26 divisions
(inc 3 Pz div)
Luftflotte I

reserve
added later
for security
operations

Eighteenth Army (Küchler)
DANZIG
KÖNIGSBERG

Fourth Panzergruppe
(Hoeppner)

Sixteenth Army
(Busch)

Third Panzergruppe
(Hoth)

Ninth Army
(Strauss)

Eighth Army
(Sobennikov)

L i t h u a n i a

North-West Front
(F.I. Kuznetsov,
then Sobennikov)
24 divisions
(inc 4 tank divs)

Eleventh Army
(Morosov)
KAUNAS

Third Army
(V.I. Kuznetsov)

SUWALKI

West Front
(Pavlov,
then Timoshenko)
38 divisions
(inc 8 tank divs)

ARMY GROUP CENTRE
51 divisions
(inc 9 Pz div)
Luftflotte II

WARSAW
Fourth Army
(Kluge)

reserve

P O L A N D

Second Panzergruppe
(Guderian)

Sixth Army (Reichenau)
KRAKOW
LUBLIN

First Panzergruppe
(Kleist)

Seventeenth Army
(Stülpnagel)

Slovakia

PRZEMYSL
LVOV

BIALYSTOK

Tenth Army
(Golubev)

MINSK
Thirteenth Army
(Filatov)
Front reserve
at Minsk

Fourth Army
(Korobkov)
BREST LITOVSK

B e l o r u s s i a

PINSK
P r i p e t   M a r s h e s
Pripet

Fifth Army
(Potapov)

ROVNO

Sixth Army
(Muzychenko)
Pre-war
Polish boundary

Twenty-sixth Army
(Kostenko)

South-West Front
(Kirponos,
then Budenny)
56 divisions
(inc 16 tank divs)

reserve

ARMY GROUP SOUTH
59 divisions
(inc 5 Pz div)
14 Rumanian
2 Hungarian
Luftflotte IV

reserve

H U N G A R Y

Hungarian
divs

CHERNOVTSY

U k r a i n e

Twelfth Army
(Ponedelin)

South Front
(Tyulenev)
16 divisions
(inc 4 tank divs)

Rum Third Army
(Dumitrescu)

Eleventh
Army
(Schobert)

Eighteenth Army
(Smirnov)

JASSY

Moldavia

R U M A N I A

Rum Fourth
Army
(Ciuperca)

Ninth Army
(Cherevichenko)

Prut

GALATI
Danube

ARMORED DIVISIONS

OTHER DIVISIONS, including motorized
infantry (in Panzergruppen) and cavalry

0   MILES   150
0   KILOMETRES   200

General Semyon Timoshenko, People's Commissar for Defence of the Soviet Union
In office: 7 May 1940 – 19 July 1941. Stalin removed him and took over the role.

Operation Barbarossa marked an escalation of the Second World War both geographically and in the formation of the Allied coalition. On Sunday, 22 June 1941, three million men of the Axis powers, the largest invasion force in the history of warfare, invaded the Soviet Union along a 1,800 mile front. In addition to troops, the Wehrmacht deployed some 600,000 motor vehicles and between 600,000 and 700,000 horses for support operations. The operation stemmed from Hitler's ideological aims to target and conquer the western Soviet Union: so that it could be repopulated by Germans for *Lebensraum* (living space); to acquire the oil reserves of the Caucasus and the agricultural resources of Soviet territories; to use the Slav peoples as slave labour, culling all inferior non-Aryan *Untermenschen* (racially inferior). Eradication of the communist ideology and european Jewry were included in the 'grand' purpose.

374ww2/2 *Feldmarschall* von Leeb, commanding **Army Group North**, plots the advance through Lithuania with *Generaloberst* Erich Hoepner, commander of *4.Panzergruppe*. Hoepner was to drive towards Leningrad.

373ww2/2 The Germans had Panzer divisions, but many German units were not mechanized. There was a mixture of foreign military and civilian vehicles used in support operations. This would create a logistical nightmare.

365ww2/2 German troops crossing the Soviet border, Sunday, 22 June 1941. The post is a border marker.

379ww2/2 A unit of Army Group North in the first days of Barbarossa moving toward Virbalis in Lithuania. The vehicle is a French Renault UE carrier, part of the war booty from France. It is being used to move an anti-tank gun and supplies.

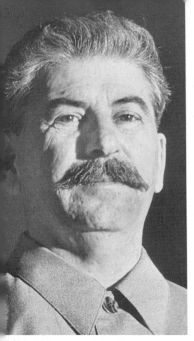

Both Britain and America were aware that the Germans were about to attack Soviet Russia. However, Stalin had signed an alliance with Hitler, the Non-Aggression Pact (August 1939) and had joined in the invasion of Poland. He was convinced that the Germans would never attack as long as they were still at war with the British. He was convinced that the British and American warnings were a conspiracy to involve the Soviet Union in a war with Germany. His own intelligence services were also reporting the same warnings, which he viewed as treasonous disinformation. It was of course impossible for the Germans to hide the massive movement of men and equipment to the eastern borders. The Germans had a cover story: the Soviets were told that the *Wehrmacht* was being deployed east beyond the range of the Royal Air Force until the invasion of Britain could be organized.

Soviet General Georgy Zhukov telephoned Stalin's house at 4.45 am on the morning of the 22 June and demanded that he be woken. There were reports of a *Luftwaffe* raid on the naval base at Sebastopol as well as other attacks. Stalin ordered Zhukov not to have the the troops respond with artillery and he was to summon a meeting of the Politburo at the Kremlin. This was convened at 5.45 am. Stalin was still convinced that Hitler was not responsible. He told Foreign Minister Molotov to summon the German ambassador, Friedrich Werner von de Schulenburg. The ambassador, who had been warned of the attack, informed Molotov that state of war existed. He was puzzled that Molotov was surprised. Molotov returned to the Politburo meeting to tell Stalin that they were at war with Germany.

372ww2/2 A panzer *abteilung* halts before another attack. A command Sd.Kfz-250 half-track heads the column July, 1941.

381ww2/2 Chief of the General Staff Georgy Zhukov woke Stalin to inform him of the attack.

371ww2/3 The tried and tested Blitzkrieg methods were employed on a much larger scale in Russia. Ju 87 dive bomber pilots were able to use their acquired skills to aid the German ground forces. Bf 109Es are escorting the Stukas.

370ww2-2 A knocked out and burning Soviet BT-7 cavalry tank, with some of its crew gunned down as they raced for cover during the early days of Operation Barbarossa.

56ww2/2 Troops of German Army Group North near Vilnius, Lithuania, 1941.

383ww2/2 Early captives taken in the opening advance of the *Wehrmacht*: a Soviet Kommissar; a civilian woman and a young soldier.

Soviet political commissars identified among captured troops were to be summarily executed as an enforcer of the Judeo-Bolshevism ideology in military forces. Protection due to prisoners of war under international law does not apply to them. When they have been separated, they are to be finished off.
An order issued by the German High Command (OKW) on 6 June 1941 before Operation Barbarossa began

367ww2/2 A motorised unit of the SS *Totenkopf* division, a formation in Army Group North, that took part in the advance through Lithuania and Latvia and by July had breached the Stalin Line.

85ww2/2 A mortar team following the rapid advance by a Panzer division.

77ww2/2 Soviet KV1 heavy tanks attempt a counter attack against the invaders.

384ww2/2 A Soviet commissar urges his comrades forward to drive the Nazi invaders back. A well-posed photograph for propaganda purposes.

376ww2/2 German troops pause to survey Russian vehicles caught on the road. The Soviet T34 medium tank came as a shock.

75ww2/2 The
existence of the T-34
and KV tanks proved
a psychological
shock to German
soldiers, who had
expected to face an
inferior enemy. The
T-34 was superior to
any tank the
Germans then had in
service. Initially, the
Germans had great
difficulty destroying
T-34s in combat, as
standard German
anti-tank weaponry
proved ineffective
against its heavy,
sloped armour.

78ww2/2 A Soviet
T-5 light, high-
speed, tank, has
crashed into the
rear of a German
Horch & Opel staff
car.

A LONE SOVIET TANK HELD UP AN ENTIRE GERMAN PANZER DIVISION

A single Soviet KV-2 held up the *6.Panzerdivision* for a day before the crew was finally overwhelmed. The tank had driven through an advancing German column and had taken up a position on a road surrounded by soft ground. It was engaged by four 50 mm anti-tank guns of the *6.Panzerdivision*. The tank was hit several times but fired back and knocked out all four enemy guns. A heavy 88 mm gun of the anti-aircraft battalion was moved up to the rear, about 800 yards behind the lone Soviet tank, but it was knocked out by the Russian tank crew before it could be loaded and fired. During the night German combat engineers tried to destroy the tank using satchel charges, but failed. Early on the morning of 25 June, German tanks fired on the KV-2 from nearby woodland, while another 88 mm anti-aircraft gun aimed at the tank's rear. Of several shots fired just two succeeded in penetrating the hull, but did not destroy it. German infantry then attacked but they were stopped by accurate machine-gun fire. Eventually the KV was knocked out by grenades thrown into the hatches. According to some accounts the dead crew were recovered and buried by the German soldiers with full military honours.

389ww2/2 A German machine gun team belonging to the 6.Panzerdivision pass one of the division's light tanks burning from a direct hit.

390ww2/2 A Soviet 45 mm anti-tank gun, model 1937, being rushed into action. The weapon was effective against German light tanks and armoured personnel carriers. Early models of the Panzer III and Panzer IV could also be knocked out at close range.

391ww2-2 The German battleship *Tirpitz* firing the 15 inch guns at the Baltic coastline in support of the German invasion of Lithuania in 1941.

393ww2/2 *Generaloberst* Erich Hoepner, commander of *4.Panzergruppe*, in discussion with *Brigadeführer* Walter Krüger, commander of the *Polizei Division*. This division had been in reserve and was to go into action against the capital and largest city of Latvia. In the fighting for the city over 2,000 of its men were killed.

392ww2/2 A knocked out Soviet T34 with its fuel tank alight and dead crewmen.

396ww2/2 General Manstein (in forage cap), commander *LVI Panzer Korps*, consulting a map with *General der Panzertruppe* Erich Brandenberger, one of his divisional commanders, in June 1941. Manstein's corps advanced rapidly, reaching the Dvina River, 196 miles distant, in just 100 hours. The assault on Luga was still underway when Manstein received orders that his next objective was to begin the advance toward Leningrad.

395ww2/2 By early July 1941 the *4.Panzergruppe* was advancing towards the ancient Russian town of Novgorod. This machine gun team is being hauled into action by its crew on the approaches to Novgorod.

396ww2/2 T34 Soviet tanks moving up for a counter attack, August 1941. *Panzergruppe* was threatening Luga, sixty-eight miles south of Leningrad. The whole of Estonia was in the process of being occupied by the German Eighteenth Army at this time.

394ww2/2 General Georgy Zhukov was made commander of the Leningrad Front on 10 September 1941. There he oversaw the defence of the city. Behind him is General Semyon Timoshenko, People's Commissar for Defence of the Soviet Union.

397ww2/2 A Soviet night patrol in camouflage smocks and armed with PPD-40 sub machine guns. By the end of the year these weapons were being replaced by the PPSh-41, a cheap, reliable, and simplified alternative to the PPD-40.

382ww2/2 Army Group North commander, Ritter von Leeb, outside h[...] HQ conferring with the commander of Sixteenth Army, *Generaloberst* Ernst Bush. The sign on the wooden hut 'Ia' indicates that the building is in use by [...] *Erster Generalstabsoffizier (Ia) (Operationen)* [First General Staff Off[...] (Operations)].

399ww2/2 The fire of anti-aircraft gun[...] deployed near St. Isaac's cathedral at t[...] beginning of the 872 days siege of Leningrad, September 1941. This was marked by the severing of the last roa[...] link. (Although the Soviet forces managed to open a narrow land corri[...] to Leningrad in January 1943.) It end[...] on 18 January 1944, making it one of [...] longest and most destructive sieges in history.

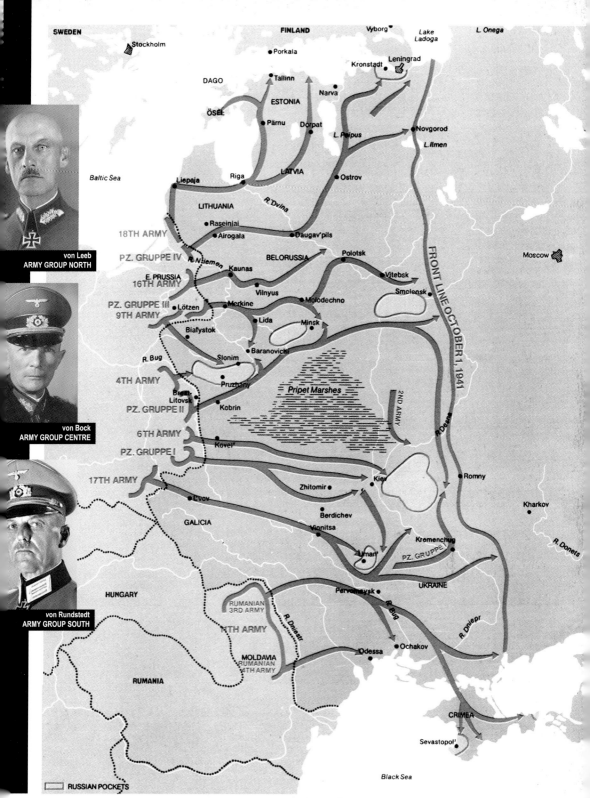

SWEDEN · FINLAND · Vyborg · Lake Ladoga · L. Onega

Stockholm · Porkala · Kronstadt · Leningrad

DAGO · Tallinn · Narva

ÖSEL · ESTONIA · Pärnu · Dorpat · L. Peipus · Novgorod · L. Ilmen

Baltic Sea · Liepaja · Riga · LATVIA · Ostrov

R. Dvina

LITHUANIA · Raseiniai

18TH ARMY · Airogala · Daugav'pils · Polotsk · Vitebsk · Moscow

PZ. GRUPPE IV · R. Niemen · BELORUSSIA · Smolensk

E. PRUSSIA · Kaunas
16TH ARMY · Vilnyus

PZ. GRUPPE III · Lötzen · Merkine · Molodechno · FRONT LINE OCTOBER 1, 1941
9TH ARMY · Lida · Minsk

Białystok

R. Bug · Slonim · Baranovichi

4TH ARMY · Pruzhany · Pripet Marshes · 2ND ARMY

Brest · Litovsk · Kobrin
PZ. GRUPPE II

6TH ARMY · Kovel'

PZ. GRUPPE I

17TH ARMY · Kiev · Romny

Lvov · Zhitomir

GALICIA · Berdichev · Kharkov
Vinnitsa · R. Donets

Kremenchug · PZ. GRUPPE

HUNGARY · Uman · UKRAINE

RUMANIAN
3RD ARMY · Pervomaysk

11TH ARMY · R. Dniestr · R. Bug · R. Dniepr

MOLDAVIA · Odessa · Ochakov
RUMANIAN
4TH ARMY

RUMANIA

CRIMEA

Sevastopol'

Black Sea

RUSSIAN POCKETS

von Leeb
ARMY GROUP NORTH

von Bock
ARMY GROUP CENTRE

von Rundstedt
ARMY GROUP SOUTH

e Soviet armies were poorly handled and frittered their tank strength away in piecemeal actions as the French had in 1940. But
e isolated Soviet troops fought with a stubbornness that the French had not shown, and their resistance caused serious problems
they pressured lines of supply long after the German tide had swept past them. By September the pincer movements of Blitzkrieg
d caught 520,000 men. These gigantic encirclements were partly the fault of Stalin who stubbornly overturned the orders of his
nerals requiring his armies to stand and fight instead of allowing them to retreat and regroup for counteroffensive operations.
tters were not helped by the mass executions of competent senior officers during the great Red Army Purges of 1936-1938.

1940-41
157

Army Group Centre's strategic goal was to defeat the Soviet armies in Belarus and occupy the city of Smolensk. To accomplish this, the army group planned for a rapid advance using Blitzkrieg operational methods, for which purpose it commanded two panzer groups rather than one. A speedy and decisive victory over the Soviet Union was expected by November 1941.

400ww2/2 An operations briefing at 3.Panzergruppe HQ. From left: *Feldmarscho* Fedor von Bock, commander of Army Group Centre; *Oberst* Walther von Hünersdo (hidden); *Generalobers* Hermann Hoth; *Luftwaffe General* Wolfram von Richthofe July 1941.

401ww2/2 *Generalobe* Heinz Guderian (right commanded 2.Panzergruppe in Ar Group Centre, under *Feldmarschall* Fedor v Bock. Guderian is in conference with the commander of the 3.Panzerdivision, *Generalleutnant* Walt Model, July 1941.Ther were six panzer divisic Guderian's command Operation Barbarossa

Feldmarshall Kesselring's *Luftflotte 2* operated in support of Army Group Centre, commanded by Fedor von Bock, continuing the close working relationship between the two commanders. Its mission was to gain air superiority while supporting ground operations. For this Kesselring had a fleet of over 1,000 aircraft, about a third of the *Luftwaffe's* total strength

403ww2/2 A recently captured Soviet airfield, where many aircraft were caught on the ground and destroyed. In the foreground is a Russian Polikarpov UTI-4, a two seater training version of the I-16 Soviet fighter. Behind the row of burnt out aircraft is a German Henschel Hs 126; the *Luftwaffe* has captured the airfield.

02ww2/2 *Generalfeldmarschall* Albert Kesselring, commander of *Luftflotte 2* supporting Army Group Centre.

05ww2/2 The Army and the *Luftwaffe* worked in close cooperation. Officers of the two services are studying reconnaissance photographs in the planning of an attack. The decoration on the officer's upper arm is the *Narvikschild* (Narvik Shield), awarded to all 577 military personnel who took part in the battles of Narvik between 9 April and 8 June 1940.

The German attack caught large numbers of Soviet Air Force aircraft on the ground. Kesselring reported that in the first week of operations *Luftflotte 2* had accounted for 2,500 Soviet aircraft in the air and on the ground. Even *Reichsmarschall* Göring found the figures hard to believe and ordered a re-check. As the ground troops advanced, the figures could be directly confirmed and were found to be too low.

406ww2/2 Heinkel 111 bombers attacking Soviet positions and vehicle convoys, 22 June 1941.

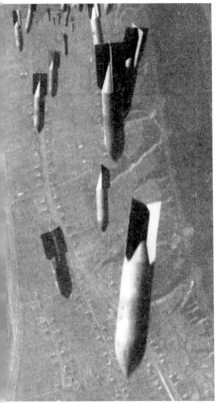

407ww2/2, 408ww2/2, 409ww2/2. Heinkel 111 bombers of KG 53 overfly an advancing German column to attack a Soviet bridge and bomb a target of opportunity: a convoy of supply trucks. Tyre tracks are evident in the fields of ripening corn, indicating where vehicles have escaped the attack.

The
Second World War
Illustrated in Colour

On the 13 September 1940 the Italian 10th Army invaded Egypt. Its goal was to seize the Suez Canal by advancing along the Egyptian coast. After many delays, the offensive was reduced to an advance of sixty miles, halting with the capture of Sidi Barrani. The Italians consolidated their gains by constructing fortified camps. The British responded with Operation Compass, a five-day raid in December 1940. It led to the collapse of the Italians and a retreat of Mussolini's 10th Army. The British pursued the remnants to El Agheila, on the Gulf of Sirte. Operation Compass was a success, with British losses at 1,900 men killed and wounded. They took 133,298 Italian and Libyan prisoners, capturing 420 tanks and over 845 guns.

2WW2/2c An Italian motorcyclist of the crack *Bersaglieri* regiment.

3WW2/2c Mussolini invaded Egypt expecting to match Hitler's conquests in Europe.

5WW2/2c In March 1941 Erwin Romme arrived in Trip with his *Afrik Korps* as a gesture from Hitler to keep Italy in the wa on the Axis si Rommel is se here with Gen Bastico. On 1 July 1941, Bas was made commander o Axis forces in North Africa. his superior, Rommel's pla had to be first approved by Bastico. The in the middle their interpre

WW2/2c A Hudson bomber of RAF Coastal Command flying over the pyramids. Egypt was one of the main bases of British operations throughout the Second World War. Around 500,000 British servicemen were there at various times, carrying on operations against the Italians and Germans, defending naval and army bases and protecting the Suez Canal.

8WW2/2c British Cruiser Mark IIA tank. The 3rd Royal Tank Regiment was equipped with these when it was posted to the Middle East. One tank commander, who went to Greece as a part of Wavell's BEF, was scathing in his criticism of this weapon: *By far their worst failing was their complete inability to move more than a mile without breaking a track or shedding one on a sharp turn... No other army would have contemplated using them.*

RITORNEREMO!

An Italian soldier of an *Alpini* unit during training. He is using a Beretta M34 semi automatic pistol. In Mussolini's invasion of Greece on 28 October 1940, the Italians had to contend with the mountainous terrain on the border and fierce resistance by the Greek Army. In two weeks the invasion was halted just inside Greek territory.

6WW2/2c An Italian propaganda postcard, issued after their defeats in Africa, with the message *We Will Return,* depicting a triumphant Italian soldier standing on British corpses, with the Union flag ripped down. It is assumed that the spectoral background image stands for the fallen Italian soldiers slain in the fighting.

11WW2/2c The Greeks stopped the Italian invasion of their country and then drove them out of Greece and back into Albania. A Greek soldier sits on a wrecked Italian *CV-33 tankette*.

2WW2/2c *Generaloberst* Maximilian on Weichs, commander of the German Second Army that invaded Yugoslavia and Greece in November 1940.

10WW2/2c German supply column halted in Greece. The vehicle at the front is a Pioneer Kw.III Light Cargo 6 x 6. Note the Swastika flags for identification from the air.

13WW2/2c A *Sturmgeschutz III* passing the foot of the Acropolis in Athens in 1941.

18WW2/2c Sunday, 27 April 1941, the German Army occupied Athens and the German flag was hoisted over the Acropolis later that morning. Note the NCO with the flare pistol ready to fire a signal when the flag reaches the top of the pole.

202ww2/2 *Generaloberst* Kurt Student planned Operation Mercury, the invasion of Crete.

21WW2/2c, 23WW2/2c, 24WW2/2c. Before the aerial assault the *Luftwaffe* attacked the anti-aircraft guns protecting the three airfields at Maleme, Retimo and Heraklion. This is a series of photographs taken of Stukas carrying out a dive bombing attack on Maleme airfield, where *Luftlande-Sturm-Regiment 1* would be brought in by Ju 52 transports. The *3.Fallschirmjäger* would be parachuted in first to overcome the defenders.

19WW2/2c Ju 52 transports preparing for Operation Mercury – the invasion of the island of Crete.

15WW2/2c, 16WW2/2c. **The Battle of Crete** was the first occasion where German paratroops were used *en masse*; the first airborne invasion in military history. The *Fallschirmjäger* were highly motivated and well trained. Their losses on Crete were such that Hitler decided in future their employment would be as conventional troops rather than airborne infantry.

4WW2/2c For the German invasion of Crete the Germans had air supremacy and were in a position to employ airborne troops. As in all theatres of war, the primary transport aircraft was the *Tante Ju* (Aunt Ju), the Junkers 52.

7WW2/2c *Fallschirmjäger* leaving a Ju 52 transport.

25WW2/2c Major General Bernard Freyberg VC, commanded the New Zealand Expeditionary Force in the Battle of Crete.

26WW2/2c British soldiers surrender to German paratroopers during the fighting on Crete.

27WW2/2c *Fallschirmjäger* in a village on Crete make use of a Morris-Commercial 15 cwt truck captured during the Battle of Crete. After the losses on Crete (5,894 casualties), Hitler decreed that the days of the airborne corps were over and directed that in future operation paratroopers were to be employed as ground-based infantry.

29WW2/2c Rommel's first act was to fly towards the enemy positions so as to familiarize himself with the terrain over which he would be fighting. He immediately disagreed with the Italian commander, General Gariboldi, over the strategic course to follow. He was not for a 'blocking operation'. After conveying his views to Rome and Berlin, he prepared to go on the offensive against the British.

28ww2/2 A *PzKpfw Mk III* being loaded on board a transport at Naples bound for Tripoli. The tank belongs to *Panzer-Regiment 5*.

30ww2/2 *PzKpfw Mk III*s deploying in the North African desert.

31WW2/2c The town gate into Bardia; Rommel captured the town in April 1941 in his opening assault to drive the British out of Libiya. Original caption: *German and Italian flags waving at the gates of Bardia. Beneath them German and Italian soldiers on guard at the town gate. They wear shorts and have rolled up their shirt sleeves. The small town shimmers white, the oleander flowers on the edge of the road and high above shines the radiant blue African sky. The staff car is a Chevrolet.

20WW2/2c Soldiers of Rommel's *Afrika Korps* resting in one of the many ruins of Byzantine churches at Apollonia, situated on the north-eastern corner of Libya at Cyrenicia. In ancient times this was a Greek colony. The German flag to identify for the *Luftwaffe* that the position has been take by German troops.

32WW2/2c Aircrews of *ZG 26* at an open-air briefing at battle headquarters.

292ww2/2 Hans-Joachim Marseille. Top *Luftwaffe* ace: al but seven of his 158 claimed victories were against the British Desert Air Force. He was killed in an accident on 3 September 1942.

4WW2/2c Bf 109E-4/N of 2.JG 27 with sand filter in front of the stoandard air intake and sporting individual camouflage paint; 1941 in Libya. he white fuselage band served as identification for aircraft used in the Mediterranean theatre.

7WW2/2c,
8WW2/2c Marseille as fêted as a hero by e Germans. He rrived in North frica in April 1941 d began his rise to claim over the next velve months until s death in 1942.

Bf 109E-4 The 'Yellow 6' was flown by Hans Joachim Marseille, who would rise in fame in 1942 to be referred to by the Germans as the 'Star of Africa'.

Marseille was the unrivalled virtuoso among the fighter pilots of the Second World War. His achievements had previously been regarded as impossible and they were never excelled by anyone after his death.

Adolf Galland, *General der Jagdflieger*

40WW2/2c A BMW R75 motorcycle sidecar combination with the *1.(leichte)Batterie / I.Abteilung / Artillerie-Regiment 155 / 21.panzerdivision*

41WW2/2c An armoured personnel carrier at a desert fort. The vehicle is a Sd Kfz 251 Aus C.

44WW2/2c Archibald Wavell, Commander-in-Chief Middle East, had been ordered to halt his advance against the Italians into Libya and send troops to Greece, where the Germans and Italians were attacking. He disagreed with this decision but followed his orders. The result was a disaster. Churchill told Wavell in June 1941 that he was to be replaced by Auchinleck. Rommel rated Wavell highly, despite Wavell's lack of success against him.

43WW2/2c A German 88 mm *Afrika Korps* gun crew working their weapon in failing light. It proved to be an effective anti tank weapon against Allied armour throughout the war.

42WW2/2c Rommel's opinion of the British commander confronting him was at variance with that of Winston Churchill, who replaced Wavell with General Sir Claude Auchinlech.

Wavell's strategic planning for the offensive had been first rate. His considerable strategic courage and sense of balance distinguished him from other British commanders, allowing him to concentrate his resources without having to consider his opponent's likely moves.

Rommel
April 1941

45WW2/2c *Afrika Korps* troops operating the MG 34 in a stationary defensi role; for this purpose the gun was mounted on a Lafette 34 tripod.

46WW2/2c Defending a desert airfield with a 20 mm Flak 30 anti aircraft gun. It had a rate of fire 120 RPM (rounds per minute).

48WW2/2c The *Bismarck* was launched in February 1939. She, along with her sister ship *Tirpitz*, were the largest battleships built by Germany, and two of the largest built by any European power. In May 1941, a German task force, consisting of the battleship *Bismarck* and the heavy cruiser *Prinz Eugen,* sailed to attack shipping in the Atlantic. However, the task force was spotted and engaged near Iceland. In the ensuing Battle of the Denmark Strait, HMS *Hood* was sunk and three other British warships were forced to withdraw. The two German ships separated. Three days later, on 27 May, the *Bismarck* was caught and sunk in the Atlantic.

9WW2/2c HMS *Hood,* early in the Battle of the Denmark Strait, was hit by several German shells and exploded. She sank within three minutes, with the loss of all but three of her crew

7WW2/2c Fairey Swordfish biplanes ('Stringbags') from the *Ark Royal* made repeated torpedo attacks and succeeded in wrecking the steering mechanism of the *Bismarck*. Battleships HMS *King George V* and HMS *Rodney* finished off the German battleship.

351ww2/2 Rudolf Hess at the Führer's side during a march past. As deputy Fuhrer, Hess was positioned behind Hermann Göring in the Nazi hierarchal succession.

On 10 May 1941, Hitler's Deputy Führer, Rudolf Hess, undertook a solo flight to Scotland, where he hoped to arrange peace talks with the Duke of Hamilton, whom he believed to be prominent in opposition to the British government. The aircraft crashed at 23:09, about twelve miles west of Dungavel House. He had planned to visit the Duke of Hamilton at his home, Dungavel House, believing – mistakenly – that the duke would be willing to negotiate peace with the Nazis on terms that would be acceptable to Hitler.

By late September 1940 it had become obvious to Hitler that the *Luftwaffe* had failed to subdue the Royal Air Force and so win mastery in the skies over southern England. Plans for the invasion of the British Isles, code named *Unternehmen Seelöwe,* were revoked. Pressure through terror bombing and the cutting off of supplies across the Atlantic was to be stepped up against Britain, forcing Winston Churchill to sue for peace. In that month the *Luftwaffe* launched an eight month campaign that would rain explosives on seventeen British cities and towns. The *Luftwaffe* gradually decreased daylight operations in favour of night attacks to evade interception by the RAF and the Blitz became a night bombing campaign after late October 1940.

52WW2/2c Göring with his Führer: his prestige had suffered a serious blow at the failure of the Luftwaffe to neutralize the Royal Air Force

WW2/2c, 54WW2/2c. A crew of a Ju 88 receiving assistance with their parachute harnesses as they prepare for a night raid on a British city.

55WW2/2c, 56WW2/2c, 57WW2/2c, 58WW2/2c, 59WW2/2c, A Heinkel 111 in a raid over London and the result for one German bomber that only just made it back to the French coast. The *Luftwaffe* launched an eight month campaign that would rain explosives on seventeen British cities and towns. The Blitz would last until May 1941, when Hitler's attention became fully concentrated on the invasion of the Soviet Union. The *Luftwaffe* gradually decreased daylight operations in favour of night attacks to evade interception by the RAF and the Blitz became a night bombing campaign after late October 1940.

64WW2/2c Thomas Alderson was a British Air Raid Precautions (ARP) warden in Bridlington. He was the first person to receive the newly-instituted George Cross from the King. The award citationds reads:

A pair of semi-detached houses at Bridlington was totally demolished in a recent air raid. One woman was trapped alive. Alderson tunnelled under unsafe wreckage and rescued the trapped person without further injury to her. Some days later, two five-storey buildings were totally demolished and debris penetrated into a cellar in which eleven persons were trapped. Six persons in one cellar, which had completely given way, were buried under debris. Alderson partly effected the entrance to this cellar by tunneling 13 to 14 feet under the main heap of wreckage and for three and a half hours he worked unceasingly in an exceedingly cramped condition. Although considerably bruised, he succeeded in releasing all the trapped persons without further injury to themselves. The wreckage was unsafe and further falls were anticipated; coal gas leaks were of a serious nature and there was danger of flooding from fractured water pipes. Despite these dangers and enemy aircraft overhead the rescue work was continued. On a third occasion, some four-storey buildings were totally demolished. Five persons were trapped in a cellar. Alderson led the rescue work in excavating a tunnel from the pavement through the foundations to the cellar; he also personally tunnelled under the wreckage many feet into the cellar and rescued alive two persons (one of whom subsequently died) from under a massive refrigerator, which was in danger of further collapse as debris was removed. Alderson worked continuously under the wreckage for five hours, during which time further air raid warnings were received and enemy aircraft heard overhead. By his courage and devotion to duty without the slightest regard for his own safety, he set a fine example to the members of his Rescue Party, and their teamwork is worthy of the highest praise.

61WW2/2c, 62WW2/2c, 63WW2/2c. Over forty towns and cities were targeted from September 1940 to May 1941. Firemen, police and ARP wardens worked constantly to rescue people and property.

A German Propaganda report concerning the invasion of Soviet Russia reads: *Squadrons of the German Luftwaffe threw darkness on the enemy turning their morning into twilight. Notwithstanding the fact that the Soviets were numerically far in the majority, on the first day on the Eastern front it had air supremacy over the Soviet Air Force in a destructive way. During that day's air combat alone, 322 Soviet aircraft were shot down by fighter pilots and by anti-aircraft artillery. The total number of destroyed Soviet aircraft had risen in the evening to 1,811 aircraft, including the aircraft destroyed on the ground. The Germans lost thirty-five aircraft on this first day.*

(From the bulletin of the German military high command concerning the first day of fighting on the Eastern Front.) Dutch language **Signaal** magazine.

84WW2/2c *Sixth Army* soldiers celebrating mass in Poland, June 1941, before the invasion of Soviet Russia. Almost all of them would not survive the battle of Stalingrad (23 August 1942 – 2 February 1943) and the captivity following the German *Sixth Army's* surrender.

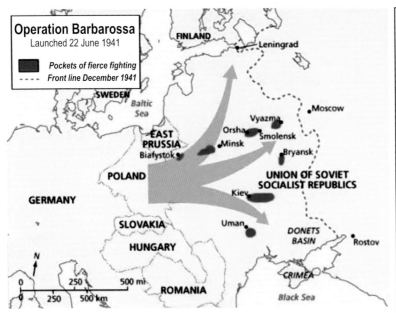

Operation Barbarossa
Launched 22 June 1941

■ Pockets of fierce fighting
---- Front line December 1941

Hans Ulrich Rudel
Stuka pilot

In early 1941, Rudel trained as a Stuka pilot and was posted to *Sturzkampfgeschwader 2*, which was moved to Poland for Operatio Barbarossa, in June 1941. On 21 September 1941, Rudel took part i an attack on the battleship *Marat* of the Soviet Baltic Fleet, which was sunk at her moorings after being hit by one 2,200 lb bomb. It caused an explosion in the forwar magazine that killed 326 men. Th *Marat's* sinking was credited to Rudel. Rudel's unit then took part Operation Typhoon, Army Group Centre''s attempt to capture Moscow. He was the most decorated German serviceman of the Second World War, being the sole recipient of the Knight's Cros with Golden Oak Leaves, Swords and Diamonds in January 1945. E the end of the war Rudel was credited with destroying: 519 tank 800 vehicles of all types; one battleship; one cruiser; 70 landing craft and 150 artillery emplacements. He claimed sever aerial victories. He flew 2,530 ground-attack missions exclusive on the Eastern Front. Post-war, h was a prominent neo-Nazi activis in Latin America and West Germany.

Feldmarschall Wilhelm von Leeb
ARMY GROUP NORTH

Feldmarschall Fedor von Bock
ARMY GROUP CENTRE

Feldmarschall Gerd von Rundstedt
ARMY GROUP SOUTH

72ww2/2c, 73ww2/2c Tried and tested Blitzkrieg methods were again employed in the attack on Soviet Russia. Stuka dive bombers returning from ground attack operations in support of the armoured led drive deep into Russia. German infantry shelter behind a Panzer III as they advance through ripening corn.

On Sunday, 22 June 1941, three million men of the Axis powers, the largest invasion force in the history of warfare, invaded the Soviet Union along a 1,800 mile front. In addition to troops, the *Wehrmacht* deployed some 600,000 motor vehicles and between 600,000 and 700,000 horses for support operations.

WW2/2c An anti-tank gun in action early in the advance.

WW2/2c A mortar team in a Russian farmyard.

WW2/2c German infantry tend a seriously wounded comrade.

WW2/2c A Soviet town under attack: a street barricade is burning
ercely after being ignited at the approach of a Panzer Mk.III. The
nk has slewed across the road, avoiding the trap.

3WW2/2c, 86WW2/2c.
Horse drawn transport
crossing a river by ford in
Russia. The bulk of the
German combat strength,
the infantry divisions,
marched into battle on
foot, with their weapons
and supply trains
propelled almost entirely
by four-legged
horsepower.

WW2/2c, 80WW2/2c.
German motorcycle troops
halted during the
advance: some having a
smoke; others, exhausted
from covering vast
distances, sleeping where
they have halted, in the
saddles of their machines

1940-41

27

87WW2/2c German infantry caught in the open and fired upon. Wounded are being attended to by a *Krankenträger* (Stretcher bearer). They wore a red cross armband and carried a pistol. There were usually four in a 1941 infantry company.

85WW2/2c Two female Soviet snipers. Between 1941–1945, a total of 2,484 Soviet female snipers were in action, mainly on the Eastern Front. Snipers of the Soviet Union played a role in slowing the rapid German advance. Officers and NCOs were the main target. Using women in this role was not the usual practice of other nations.

3WW2/2c Type VIIB U-boats heading for the open
as from their captured bases in the Bay of Biscay,
 the west coast of France.

WW2/2c An Allied merchant ship under attack by
 ̃ocke Wulf bomber. These aircraft had the
 ditional task of locating convoys and signalling
 eir position to the U-boats.

WW2/2c Karl Dönitz at the start of the Second
 orld War, was the senior submarine officer in the
 iegsmarine. In January 1943, he achieved the rank
 Großadmiral and replaced Grand Admiral Erich
 eder as Commander-in-Chief of the Navy. On 30
 ril 1945 Dönitz was named Hitler's successor as
 ad of state, with the title of President of Germany.

WW2/2c A Royal Air Force Hawker Hurricane Mk
 on the catapult of a CAM (Catapult Armed
 rchant) ship. In spite of heavy losses and the one-
 ght-only waste of aircraft, the catapult ships
 nained in service until 1943. They were a defence
 inst Focke Wulf Condor aircraft.

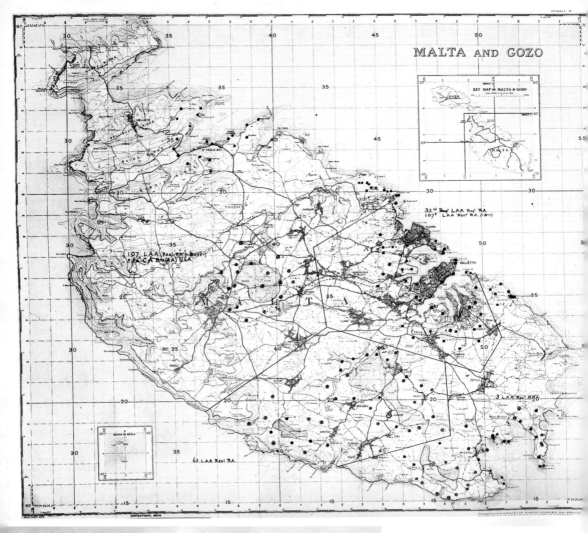

MALTA AND GOZO

93WW2/2c An obvious target for an aerial bombardment, the island had many guns sited in four defence zones, especially sited to defend the airfields, harbour and potential coastal invasion beaches.

The Siege of Malta lasted two and a half yea from 1940–42; the struggle for control of th strategically important island of Malta, then British colony, pitted the air forces and navies Italy and Germany against the Royal Air For and the Royal Navy. The opening of a new fro in North Africa in June 1940 enhanced Malta already immense value to both the Allies and t Axis forces.

60WW2/2 A 40 mm Bofors anti-aircraft gun protecting the Grand Harbor at Valletta, Malta, 1940. The weapon is located in Upper Barrakka Gardens, looking towards Fort St Michael. The sie of the British colony began in June 1940 and aeri attacks would last two and a half years.

194WW2/2c *Generalfeldmarschall* Albert Kesselring sharing a light-hearted moment with the crew of a Ju 88. (Perhaps the joke concerned the boy-like appearance of a crew member.) Kesselring, in 1941, was appointed *Wehrmacht* Commander-in-Chief South and was transferred to Italy. He succeeded in establishing local air superiority and neutralised Malta, which provided a base from which British aircraft and submarines could intercept Axis convoys headed for North Africa.

196WW2/2c Bf 110s flying out of Sicily and heading for Malta to target the Allied shipping servicing the island fortress.

195WW2/2c A warship of the Royal Navy escorts a merchant vessel carrying vital cargo for the islanders and defenders.

The war against France and Great Britain has been running two years; the USSR is resisting stubbornly and the matter needs to be settled before winter sets in. The German Führer will decide where his blows in the east must fall next in order to bring about a victorious end for the Fatherland.

ww2/2 Refuelling a Ju 87B. Stuka squadrons 1, 2 and 77 operated almost continually against Soviet positions and individual targets. Summer 41 on the Army Group Centre front.

ww2/2 German infantry taken forward on Panzer III tanks during the thrust towards Smolensk.

413ww2./2 A German column led by a Panzer IV near Vitebsk during the First Battle of Smolensk in July 1941.

414ww2/2 Soldiers of the 20th Soviet Army fighting on the banks of the River Dnieper to the west of Dorogobuzh.

12ww2/2 Jaws of a massive German pincer movement sought to close and cut off three Soviet Armies (16, 19 and 20) east of Smolensk.

The fighting for the capture of the city of Smolensk took place between 10 July and 10 September 1941, about 250 miles west of Moscow. The *Wehrmacht* had advanced 410 miles into the USSR in the eighteen days after the onset of Operation Barbarossa on 22 June 1941. The Germans encountered unexpected resistance during the battle for Smolensk, leading to a two month delay in their advance on Moscow. Three Soviet armies, the 16, 19 and 20, were encircled and destroyed to the north of Smolensk; though a significant number of men from 19 and 20 armies managed to escape eastwards from the pocket.

16ww2/2 The Russian soldier was putting up stiff resistance to formations of Army Group Centre.

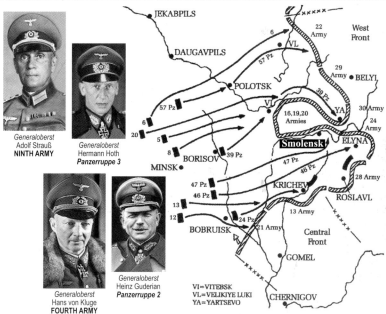

Generaloberst
Adolf Strauß
NINTH ARMY

Generaloberst
Hermann Hoth
Panzerruppe 3

Generaloberst
Hans von Kluge
FOURTH ARMY

Generaloberst
Heinz Guderian
Panzerruppe 2

VI = VITEBSK
VL = VELIKIYE LUKI
YA = YARTSEVO

417ww2/2 A Soviet counter attack during the fighting near Smolensk.

423ww2/2 A German anti-tank gun crew manning a 3.7 cm Pak 36 during the advance towards the Stalin Line, August 1941. The weapon was proving ineffective against the Soviet medium and heavy tanks. The German soldier had taken to calling the weapon 'the door knocker'.

22ww2/2 In the outskirts of Vitebsk German infantry halt to take refreshment during fighting for the city, 22 August 1941. Hoth's *Panzergruppe* drove north and then east, taking Polotsk and Vitebsk.

24ww2/2 The more effective German anti-tank weapon, the 88 mm gun that could punch a hole through most Allied tank armour – nicknamed by its crews 'the can opener'.

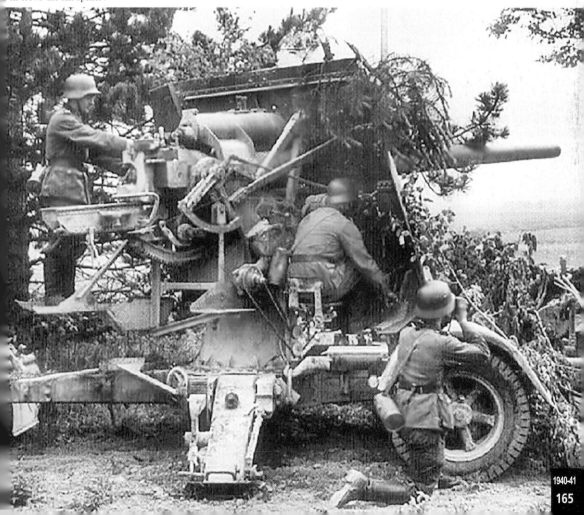

428ww2/2 SS-*Obergruppenführer* Paul Hausser commanding the SS-*Reich* division part of *XXXXVI Korps*, fought with Army Group Centre, taking part in the Battle of Yelnya near Smolensk.

427ww2/2 Troops of the SS-*Reich* (later renamed *Das Reich*) operating a an anti-tan gun, the Pak 38. The Pak 38 was first used against Soviet tanks in 1941 during Operatic Barbarossa. It was one of the few early guns capable of penetrating the 45 mm (1.8 in) sloped armor of the T-34's hull at close rang

426ww2/2 A severely wounded Russian crewman lies beside his knocked out T34 while a seemingly unsympathetic German n looks on.

429ww2/2 General Fyodor Kuznetsov, commander of the 51st Independent Army, later serving as the temporary commander of the Central Front (July–August 1941), Chief of Staff of the 28th Army.

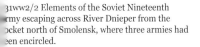

430ww2/2 A Russian position on the banks of the Dnieper captured by the Germans during the advance on Smolensk.

431ww2/2 Elements of the Soviet Nineteenth Army escaping across River Dnieper from the pocket north of Smolensk, where three armies had been encircled.

34ww2/2 Cheerful defenders
f the City of Smolensk.

25ww2/2 German soldiers
uring a pause in the fighting
lenching their thirsts from a
ucket of water. This was taken
uring the fighting to trap the
oviet armies north of
molensk.

33ww2/2 An action
hotograph taken during the
erman attack on the
erimeter defence ring on the
pproaches to Smolensk.

25ww2/2 Russian soldiers
urrendering to the victorious
ermans.

438ww2/2 A German soldier wounded during the mopping-up operations in the Smolensk area, July-August 1941. German wounded numbered 100,327 in the fighting around Smolensk.

436ww2/2,437ww2/2 Russian captives being rounded up. On 27 July, the two arms of the Germans pincer linked up and closed the pocket east of Smolensk, trapping large portions of Sixteenth, Nineteenth and Twentieth Armies. Approximately 300,000 men were taken prisoner. Many would die in captivity. During the Second World War, Nazi Germany engaged in a policy of deliberate maltreatment of Soviet prisoners of war, in contrast to their treatment of British and American prisoners. This resulted in some 3.3 to 3.5 million deaths. Most died during the death marches from the front lines or under inhumane conditions in German prisoner of war camps and concentration camps.

32ww2/2 Two Russian escaped crewmen from a destroyed T34 await capture. Prior to the German attack, the Soviets launched a counter-offensive; in July, the 7th and 5th Mechanized Corps of the Soviet Twentieth Army attacked with 1,500 tanks. The result was a disaster, as the offensive ran directly into the anti-tank defences of the German 7th Panzer Division and the two Soviet mechanized corps were badly mauled.

The Battle of Smolensk was a severe defeat for the Soviet Army in the opening phase of Operation Barbarossa and a success for Army Group Centre. For the first time, the Soviets tried to implement a coordinated counter-attack against a large part of the front; although this was a failure, the increasing stiff resistance showed that the Russians were by no means defeated and that the advance towards Moscow was not going to be an easy undertaking.

On the day Smolensk fell Senior Lieutenant Yakov Dzhugashvili, commander of an artillery battery in the VII Mechanized Corps, was captured east of Vitebsk. Yakov was Stalin's son by his first wife, Ekaterina Svanidze, who died in 1907 from tuberculosis. Later in the war the Germans proposed to exchange Yakov for *Feldmarschall* Friedrich Paulus, captured at Stalingrad in 1943. Stalin turned down the offer, allegedly stating: 'I do not trade lieutenants for field marshals'. Shortly thereafter, Yakov committed suicide in a PoW camp by charging the wire. He was shot dead by a German guard.

439ww2-2, 440ww2/2, 441ww2/2.
Photographs taken of elements of the 29.*division* (motorized) troops fighting in the vicinity of Smolensk. On the morning of 16 July 1941, the Germans renewed the attack and even though the defenders fought tenaciously the German 29.*division* was in possession of Smolensk by that evening.

442ww2/2 Adolf Hitler arriving by Ju 52 to visit *Feldmarschall* Gerd von Rundstedt at the headquarters of **Army Group South**. Rundstedt shakes hands with the Führer.

The Ukraine was a main area of Soviet industry and mining. It was also a large farming part of the USSR. This was the land require by Hitler for his plans for *Lebensraum* (living space). Army Group South was to advance up to the River Volga, engaging and drawin in a large part of the Red Army in battle, thus leaving the way for the Army Group North, with the prize of Leningrad, and Army Grou Centre to take Moscow. To carry out these initial tasks its battle order included the First Panzer Group (*Feldmarschall* Ewald von Kleis and the German Sixth Army (*Feldmarschall* Walter von Reichenau); the Seventeenth Army (*Generalleutnant* Carl-Heinrich vo Stülpnagel) and Eleventh Army (*Generaloberst* Ritter von Shobert); *Luftlotte 4* (*Generaloberst* Alexander Löhr) and the Romania Third and Fourth Armies.

445ww2-2 Heinz Guderian at a forward command post for one of his panzer regiments near Kiev, 1941. After his armoured spearhead captured Smolensk, Guderian's panzer group was ordered to turn south to encircle the Soviet forces to the south at Kiev. In September 1941 Guderian was ordered to make a drive for Moscow. Note the curious Russian family looking on at the foreign invaders.

443ww2/2 *Generaloberst* Alexander Löhr, Austrian commander of *Luftlotte 4*.

444ww2/3 Alexander Löhr with *Generalmajor* Wolfram von Richthofen, commanding *Fliegerkorps VIII*.

450ww2/2 *Luftflotte 4* operated with Army Group South, tasked with assisting ground attack operations across South East Poland, the Ukraine towards the City of Kiev and the River Dnieper. Do 17 bombers on a bombing mission.

446ww2/2 A part of the city of Kiev totally destroyed in the bombing. Much of the Southwestern Front of the Red Army (commanded by General Mikhail Kirponos) fought to defend the city but was encircled.

447ww2/2 Men from a German forward detachment attack a Soviet village west of Kiev in August 1941.

453ww2/2 Knocked out T-26 light tanks of the Soviet 19th Tank Division near the Vojnitsa-Lutsk highway. Interestingly, the turrets are turned to the rear, which suggests a surprise attack from that quarter. The T-26 was the most numerous tank in the Red Army's armoured force during the German invasion. It was a development of the British Vickers Mark E and was licensed by the Soviets as the T-26.

454ww2/2 A Soviet mortar team, armed with 120 mm mortars, moving to new defence lines on the Southwestern Front, August 1941.

451ww2/2 General Mikhail Petrovich Kirponos, Soviet commander of the Southwestern Front. Unlike so many Soviet commanders, Kirponos acted on the intelligence reports of an iminent Nazi invasion and his command was alert on 22 June when the Germans attacked. He was killed in action during the defence of Kiev, 20 September 1941.

455ww2/2 A German StuG III Assault gun; this mounted a 75 mm gun. They were employed as infantry support and mobile artillery.

452ww2/2 A section of the battlefield at Brody; a Soviet anti-tank unit caught in the open and wiped out.

457ww2/2 Marshal of the Soviet Union Semyon Mikhailovich Budyonny.

From July to September 1941, Marshal Budyonny was in command at Kiev, the capital of the Ukraine. His task was to hold the city while evacuating industrial machinery. Seeing plainly that they were going to be encircled by the Germans, the cavalryman urged Stalin to allow a retreat. Stalin forbade it. The disaster which followed the German encirclement cost the Soviet Union 1.5 million men killed or taken prisoner. It was one of the largest encirclements in military history. Stalin made Budyonny the scapegoat, dismissing him as commander-in-chief and replacing him with Timoshenko. A staggering 665,000 Red Army soldiers were lost as prisoners to the Germans,

456ww2/2 Budyonny was a notable horse-breeder, who had insisted that the tank could never replace the horse as an instrument of war.

461ww2/2 Soviet cavalry crossing the River Ugra near Yelnya, east of Smolensk, as the panzers closed the pincers of the pocket to the west of the city, July 1941.

458ww2/2 A Soviet T-26 light tank with five dead Russian soldiers. The crew consisted of three: commander, gunner and driver; the others could be executed prisoners.

63ww2/2 German infantry with their supporting StuG I Assault gun.

466ww2/2 Red Army artillery team firing a ML-20, 152 mm howitzer, July 1941.

45ww2/2 Russians watch German preparations to make a river crossing.

516ww2/2, 517ww2/2, 518ww2/2, 513ww2/2. Crossing the Dnieper river in the late summer of 1941 using the Flossacke 34 Assault Inflatable Boats. For speed during daylight operations an outboard motor could be attached.

The *1.SS Panzerdivision Leibstandarte Adolf Hitler* began as Adolf Hitler's personal bodyguard, responsible for guarding the Führer's person, offices, and residences. Initially the size of a regiment, the LSSAH eventually grew into an elite division-sized formation. For Operation Barbarossa it was under the command of Gerd von Rundstedt's Army Group South and took part in the Battle of Uman and the capture of Kiev.

521ww2/2 *SS Gruppenführer* Josef Dietrich, commander of the LSSAH. Despite having no formal military staff officer training, Dietrich was, the highest-ranking officer in the Waffen-SS, reaching the rank of *Oberst-Gruppenführer,*

519ww2/2 Soviet soldiers taken by men of the Waffen SS division, *1.panzerdivision Leibstandarte SS Adolf Hitler*, (LSSAH). One prisoner appears to be taking exception to the camera and his comrade seems to be warning him to shut up.

522ww2/2 a patrol of the LSSAH in a forest in the sector of XIV Corps, Arm Group South, summer 1941.

The *1.SS Panzerdivision Leibstandarte SS Adolf Hitler*

523ww2/2 A machine gun team of the Leibstandarte during the advance into Soviet Russia, August 1941.

525ww2/2 Soviet infantry attacking through shell fire. The weapon being carried is the PTRD 41 (*ProtivoTankovoye Ruzhyo Degtyaryova*) anti-tank rifle. It was used from early 1941.

532ww2/2 Soviet infantry, who had been taking cover in a corn field, surrender to the *Leibstandarte*.

24ww2/2 A Leibstandarte MG 34 team approaching Russian positions dug in by the Dneiper river. An artillery spotter is using an optical rangefinder, model EM34. It proved to be very effective and was used extensively by German mobile artillery ground units. The optics were so far advanced for the time that gave the Germans a decided advantage over Allied forces.

530ww2/2 The original caption: *The machine gunner – the backbone of the infantry's firepower in battle.*

31ww2/2 A Soviet mortat team knocked out in the August ghting. The weapon is the RM-38, a 50 mm light infantry ortar.

533ww2/2 SS *Sturmbannführer* Kurt Meyer commanded a reconnaissance detachment of the *Leibstandarte* in 1941.

534ww2/2 Men of the SS *Leibstandarte* advancing into the outskirsts of a Russian town, August 1941.

38ww2/2 An unidentified SS unit with three light machine guns, 'G 34s, passing through a Russian village.

540ww2/2 *SS Obergruppenführer* Paul Hausser commanded *2.SS-Panzerdivision 'Das Reich'*.

541ww2/2 A *Das Reich*, 8 x 8 heavy armoured car (Sd. Kfz.252) in the thick forests near Chominski.

2.SS-Panzerdivision 'Das Reich'. The *Das Reich* fought with Army Group Centre during Operation Barbarossa.

548ww2/2 SS *Obergruppenführer* Theodor Eicke commanded *3.SS-Panzerdivision 'Totenkopf'*.

549ww2/2 Soldiers of the SS *Totenkopf Division* seen here resting in a burning village during the summer of 1941. The vehicle is a Kfz.15 Horch.

550ww2/2 SS *Obergruppenführer* Walter Krüger took command of *4.SS-Polizei Division* when Arthur Mülverstedt was killed in August

551ww2/2 An armoured, half track personnel carrier designed to accompany tanks and transport troops into battle.

3.SS-Panzerdivision 'Totenkopf'. The *Totenkopf* (death's head) division drew most of its initial personnel from concentration camp guards (*SS-Totenkopfverbände*). Others were added from German militia units.

4.SS-Polizei Division. Its personnel wer not enrolled in the SS and remained policemen, retaining their structure and insignia. By so doing it provided a mean for policemen to avoid army conscription.

35ww2/2 SS *Gruppenführer* Felix Martin Julius Steiner commanded *SS-Panzerdivision 'Wiking'*.

36ww2/2 A PzKw Mk III tank of the *Wiking Division* in the Soviet Union August 1941.

552ww2/2 SS *Oberführer* Carl-Maria Demelhuber commanded *6.SS-Gebirgs Division 'Nord'*.

554ww2/2 The German mountain troops joined with the Finns in fighting the Soviets in the Artic Circle. However, the SS component was unprepared for arctic warfare and suffered heavy casualties.

5.SS-Panzerdivision 'Wiking'. The *Wiking division* recruited from foreign volunteers in Denmark, Norway, Sweden, Finland, Estonia, Holland and Belgium, with German officers commanding.

6.SS-Gebirgs Division 'Nord'. The *Nord* was formed by volunteers from Hungary, Romania, and Norway. It was the only Waffen-SS unit to fight in the Arctic Circle, when stationed in Finland and Russia.

560ww2/2 Soviet militiamen surrender to SS soldiers in Ju[l]
1941. Within minutes of this picture being taken both
prisoners were shot out of hand as they were captured
fighting in civilian clothing.

558ww2/2 A *Wehrmacht* soldier proceeds with caution as h[e]
searches outbuildings of a farm, Luger pistol in hand.

559ww2/2 Russan peasants pressed into service by the
invaders to assist motorcyclists of the SS *Reich Division*,
struggling in the Russian mud. Curious villagers observe at
first hand the invaders' determination to occupy their
country.

557ww2/2 Wehrmacht infantry bringing death and
destruction to the Russian people, their property and
belongings.

56ww2/2 Their shelter and livlihoods shattered, these Russian peasants salvage what they can from their burning village.

55ww2/2 German motorcyclists and Ukrainian civilians near Rovno, July 1941. Facial expressions that appear to convey emotions of anticipated carnal pleasure, youthful disappoval, fearful apprehension and childish bewilderment.

526ww2/2 An NCO of the *Wehrmacht* is about to carry out the execution of two captured women of the Red Army. They have been taken back to the gun pit where they had been operating a machine gun from – the hole would serve as their grave. German Army guidelines for the *Conduct of the Troops in Russia* issued by the OKW on 19 May 1941, directed: *ruthless and vigorous measures against Bolshevik inciters, guerrillas, saboteurs, Jews and the complete elimination of all active and passive resistance.* Influenced by these guidelines, the regular armed forces, represented by the *Wehrmacht,* committed countless war crimes.

527ww2/2 German soldiers engaged in operations near Kherson against Soviet partisans among the waterways of the Dneiper estuary in the summer of 1941.

While engaged in 'anti-bandit' (*Bandenbekämpfung*) operations, the *Wehrmacht* took part in the massacre of Russian Jews. Its co-operation with the SS in anti-partisan and anti-Jewish operations was close. *Feldmarschall* Walther von Brauchitsch ordered, when Operation Barbarossa began, that all German Army commanders were to identify and register all Jews in the occupied areas in the Soviet Union at once and to co-operate fully with the *Einsatzgruppen*. The *Einsatzgruppen* in front-line areas were to operate under Army command while the Army would provide assistance to the murder squads, including all necessary logistical support.

528ww2/2 German soldiers engaged in operations against Soviet partisans among the waterways of the Dneiper estuary in the summer of 1941.

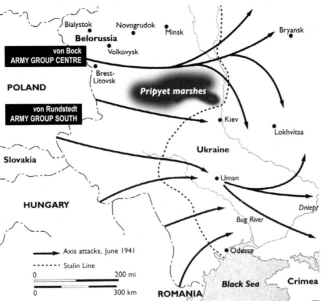

During the invasion of the Soviet Union, the German armies skirted the wetlands, passing through the north or south of it. The marshes divided the central and southern theatres of operation during the Second World War. The marshes served as a sanctuary for both Soviet and Polish partisans. Known as *Pripjet-Sümpfe* by the Germans, the wetlands were dreaded by the *Wehrmacht* troops and numerous attempts were made to flush the area of partisan fighters.

Our motor column had to make six stops owing to sabotaged bridges; four times we were halted by small arms fire. The stop between Slinim and Baranovichi was particularly long, for we were ordered to repair a big bridge there, destroyed by guerillas two hours before. We hardly made twenty kilometres before we ran into heavy fire again and this went on until we got out of the forest. As a result four men were killed and three wounded in our vehicle. We did not stop fighting these invisible attackers until we got to the front. In the proximity of Berezino we fought a pitched battle with them. As a result our company lost forty men.

Gefreiter Gra[...]
445.infanterie regime[...]

460ww2/2 Russian partisans had begun operations against the Germans behind their front lines by August – September time. The massive wetland offered cover for their highly effective nuisance activities. The partisan is taking the slain German machine gunner's MG 34 weapon. He is already carrying a German MP 40 machine pistol (*Maschinenpistole 40*). It was often erroneously called the 'Schmeisser' by the Allies, although weapon designer Hugo Schmeisser was not involved in its design or production.

8ww2/2, 469ww2/2 Soviet guerillas operating behind the eastward advancing Germans caused severe disruption to the lines of supply. Men are en here laying explosive charges under railway tracks. Explosive charges were not always easy to come by and effective explosive material were tracted from artillery shells. All four men are armed with Soviet PPSh M 1941 submachine guns. It was one of the major infantry weapons of the oviet Armed Forces. Around six million PPSh-41s were manufactured. A German light aircraft overflies and photographs the damage to one of the any results of efficient handiwork of the irregular forces operating behind the front.

562ww2/2 Partisans resting in the vast and dense forests of central Russia. There are at least five women in this photograph. Weapons and equipment evident are both Russian and captured German. A directive from the OKW (Oberkommando der Wehrmacht) stated: '*For the life of on* *German soldier, a death sentence of from fifty to one hundred Communists must be generally deemed commensurate*'. These terror tactics only served to swell the ranks of the partisans, as both men and women were driven to flee for their lives into the wildness areas.

563ww2/2 *Feldgendarmerie* operating in occupied Russia, July 1941. The sign reads: 'Partisan danger ahead. Single vehicles Stop! Hold weapons ready.' Lone transports were instructed to wait for a convoy. *Feldgendarmerie* were employed within army divisions and as self-contained units under the command of an army corps. They worked in close cooperation with the *Geheime Feldpolizei* (Secret Field Police), district commanders and the SS.

Wehrmacht 'Ringkragen' Feldgendarmerie gorget.

61ww2/2 A captured partisan with minutes left to live; after interrogation by the these officers of the *Feldgendarmerie* he will be taken out and shot – or hung by the neck.

64ww2/2 Partisans hung by the Germans as a deterent for those considering resistance.

57ww2/2 A German speaking Russian officer questions a captured German prisoner and seems to have evoked a spirited response.

66ww2/2 Soviet officers taking a break from interrogating a captured German soldier south of Voronezh, 1941. Both sides were playing rough.

470ww2/2 Nurse Masha Bruskina to hang.

On 26 October, 1941, three partisans were hanged in Minsk, perhaps the first of such public execution of resistance members of the war. Seventeen years old Maria (Masha) Bruskina was the central figure of the grim ceremony. She was a Belarusian Jewish nurse and member of the Minsk Resistance who had managed to hide her Jewish identity. While volunteering as a nurse, she cared for wounded Soviet soldiers and assisted them in escaping. One eye-witness account:

Before noon, I saw the armed German and Lithuanian soldiers appear on the street. From over the bridge they escorted three people with their arms tied behind their backs. In the middle there was a girl with a sign-board on her chest. They were led up to the yeast factory gate. I noticed how calmly these people walked. The girl did not look around. The first one to die was the girl.

She was hanged with unshaven First World War veteran Kiril Trus and a sixteen year old youngster, Volodia Shcherbatsevich. The men were members of a partisan cell organizing anti-fascist resistance; Masha Bruskina was a nurse who had been caught aiding the partisans by providing civilian clothes and papers for wounded Red Army soldiers under her care and to smuggle them to join the ranks of the resistance fighters. Shades of Edith Cavell, the British nurse shot by the Germans for similar activites in the Great War. Twelve resistance fighters were hanged at Minsk that day.

471ww2/2 The captured partisans were led through the streets of Minsk to the execution site. A Wehrmacht officer of the *707.Infanterie Division* acted as hangman. The board hanging from the girl's neck reads in both German and in Russian, *We guerrillas fired on German troops.*

472ww2/2 The officer fixes the noose. Masha resisted attempts to make her face the crowd.

473ww2/2 The sixteen year old youngster, Volodia Shcherbatsevich, appears to be addressing words to the dying Masha as he is being prepared for hanging by the same German officer.

76ww2/2 The same executioner moves on to his final victim, the older partisan, Kiril Trus. The bodies were left hanging on the makeshift gibbet at the yeast factory for three days as a warning to any who would resist the invaders.

77ww2/2 Rather than discourage resistance by the civilian population, harsh measures served to swell the ranks of the fighters. Dense woods and marshes proved to be effective hiding places for escaped soviet prisoners of war, Polish partisans and Jews fleeing the Nazi extermination measures being waged against them. The guerilla fighters were not short of targets behind the advancing German lines.

478ww2/2 SS-*Standartenführer*
Hermann Fegelein. His command in 1941
murdered over 17,000 civilians during the
Pripyat swamps punitive operations.

480ww2/2 SS-*Obergruppenführer* Erich von dem
Bach-Zelewski. He was appointed by Himmler and
oversaw the extermination of Jews in Riga and Minsk
by the *Einsatzgruppe B.*

481ww2/2 *Reichsführer* Heinrich Himmler.
formed the *Einsatzgruppen* and built
extermination camps. Himmler directed the
killing of some six million Jews.

In early August 1941, Himmler ordered the *SS-Kavallerie-Brigade* to be formed and to undertake, under the general command of vo
dem Bach, the systematic combing and clearing of the Pripyat marshes. Enemy soldiers in uniform were to be taken prisoner, an
those found out of uniform were to be shot. Jewish males, with the exception of a few skilled workers such as doctors and leathe
workers, would be shot. Himmler was not satisfied with the results and called for all male Jews over the age of fourteen to be killed
Women and children were to be driven into the swamps and drowned. Thus Fegelein's units were among the first in the Holocaust t
wipe out entire Jewish communities. As the water in the swamps was too shallow and some areas had no swamps, it proved impractica
to drown the women and children, so in the end they were also shot. At the time of Fegelein taking command the brigade had
strength of 3,500 men, 2,900 horses and 375 vehicles.

479ww2/2 Fegelein's cavalry during operations in the Pripyat marshes. His final report on the operation, dated 18 September 1941, stated that the
killed 14,178 Jews, 1,001 partisans, and 699 Red Army soldiers with losses of seventeen dead, thirty-six wounded and three missing.

83ww2/2 A Wehrmacht unit on patrol to root out partisan fighters in the marshlands. They are wearing mosquito nets over their faces.

82ww2/2 German soldiers rounding up Russian civilians who might be used by them as hostages and shot in reprisal when German soldiers had been attacked. Jews were often shot immediately.

84ww2/2 In this instance when the shooting of Jewish women and children began one woman appears to be making a dash for it clutching her child.

485ww2/2 Reichführer Himmler inspects a prisoner of war camp in Russia 1941. The problem of feeding so many captives was easily taken care of by ignoring the issue.

490ww2/2 Caught by the camera enjoying his work, the nearest SS killer has fired his first shot into the left shoulder of his victim. His next shot, presumably, will be into the man's head.

488ww2/2 German soldiers of the Waffen-SS and the Reich Labour Service look on as a member of *Einsatzgruppe D* prepares to shoot a Ukrainian Jew kneeling on the edge of a mass grave filled with corpses.

Einsatzgruppen (task forces)

Created by Himmler and under the supervision of Heydrich, the *Einsatzgruppen* operated in territories occupied by the Wehrmacht, following in the wake of the fighting troops. They were charged with rounding up and killing Jews via firing squad and gas vans. Historian Raul Hilberg estimates that between 1941 and 1945 the *Einsatzgruppen* and related auxiliary troops killed more than two million people, including 1.3 million Jews.

486ww2/2 *SS-Gruppenführer* Reinhard Heydrich organized the *Einsatzgruppen*.

491ww2/2 Polish women being led to a mass execution site near the village of Palmiry in the Kampinos Forest, northwest of Warsaw. Between December 1939 and July 1941 more than 1,700 Poles and Jews – mostly inmates of Warsaw's Pawiak prison – were executed by the SS and *Ordnungspolizei* in a forest glade near Palmiry.

489ww2/2 An *Einsatzgruppen* unit in action in the Soviet Union, employing a variation in method of shooting helpless victims.

487ww2/2 *SS-Brigadeführer* Otto Ohlendorf, *Einsatzgruppen D*. By the end of the war his unit had killed 90,000 men, women and children.

465ww2/2 Marshal Ion Antonescu,
Conducător of Romania.

On 12 June 1941, during a summit with Hitler, Ion Antonescu first learned of the special nature of Operation Barbarossa, namely, that the war against the Soviet Union was to be an ideological war to annihilate the forces of 'Judo-Bolshevism'. It was to be a war of extermination to be executed without mercy. Antonescu was shown a copy of *Richtlinien für das Verhalten der Truppen in Russland* (Guidelines for the Conduct of the Troops in Russia), that Hitler had issued to his forces concerning the special treatment to be meted out to Soviet Jews. The Hitler-Antonescu friendship was remakable in that neither could speak the others language. Hitler only knew German while the other language Antonescu spoke was French, in which he was fluent. Antonescu totally accepted Hitler's ideas about Operation Barbarossa as a race war. He instantly began taking punitive measures against Jewish citizens in Romania. Romania joined the attack on the Soviet Union, led by Germany in coalition with Hungary, Finland, the State of Slovakia, the Kingdom of Italy and the Independent State of Croatia.

464ww2/2 The Romanian leader, Antonescu and Adolf Hitler at the Führerbau in Munich June 1941, before Operation Barbarossa. German Foreign Minister Joachim von Ribbentrop and *Generalfeldmarschall* Wilhelm Keitel are behind them. Antonescu issued the order, dated June 22, 1941, committing Romania to invade the Soviet Union and retake Bessarabia and Northern Bukovina.

92ww2/2 Jews of Iaşi being rounded up and arrested during the pogrom.

93ww2/2 A Jewish family of Iaşi murdered in the street of the town.

The Iaşi pogrom was a series of actions by forces under Marshal Ion Antonescu in the Romanian city of Iaşi against its Jewish community. It lasted from 29 June to 6 July 1941. According to Romanian authorities, over 13,266 people, or one third of the Jewish population, were massacred. One method of cruel killing by the Romanian authorities was by train: In the death train that left Iaşi for Călăraşi, southern Romania, which carried perhaps as many as 5,000 Jews, only 1,011 reached their destination alive after eight days.

94ww2/2 As many as 100 people were stuffed into each cattle truck. Many died of thirst, starvation, and suffocation aboard two trains that for eight days travelled back and forth across the countryside. The dead are being unloaded at one stop.

The Romanian military force engaged in Operation Barbarossa formed a **General Antonescu Army Group** under the effective command of German general, *Generaloberst* Eugen Ritter von Schobert, commander of the German Eleventh Army.

Romania's campaign on the Eastern Front began without any formal declaration of war. It was launched by Antonescu's statement: ***Soldiers, I order you, cross the Prut River!***

On 22 June 1941 the Romanian Third Army comprised: the IV Army Corps (6th and 7th Infantry Divisions); the Cavalry Corps (5th and 8th Cavalry Brigades); the Mountain Corps (1st, 2nd, and 4th Mountain Brigades); two separate artillery battalions; a target acquisition battery and the Romanian Air Force's 3rd Army Cooperation Command.

498ww2/2 Lieutenant General Nicolae Ciupercă commanded the Romanian Fourth Army.

496ww2/2 A Romanian soldier accepts a light for his cigarette from a German panzer crewman. A propaganda photograph, showing men of the Axis forces working together to defeat the Soviet army.

499ww2/2 *Generaloberst* Eugen Ritter von Schobert. The Romanian forces were under the command of his Eleventh Army. He died on 12 Sepetember 1941 in flying accident when his Fieseler Storch came down in a Russian mine field.

97ww2/2 In September 1941, a Romanian cavalry unit crossing a pontoon bridge over the River Pruth, which formed Romania's border with Moldova and Ukraine.

100ww2/2 Marshal Ion Antonescu with his staff during the Axis advance into the Ukraine. A German liason officer, presumably Romanian or French speaking, as Antonescu did not speak German, consults maps with them. The vast terrain would soon appear to swallow the invaders up the further they advanced.

5ww2/2 Romanian infantry during the summer advance take cover in a field ripe for harvesting.

507ww2/2 Original caption: *Men of a Romanian armoured unit are anxiously awaiting the attack command.* The automatic pistol is an Austrian Steyr M12.

512ww2/2 Original caption: *A heavy motorized battery, which tried to escape during the hasty withdrawal of Soviet troops, was caught in the middle of the city, thanks to rapid intervention.*

511ww2/2 Original caption: *In front of us a few motorcyclists, behind us comes a second tank and then a few motorcycles follow - so we drive up the hill. Just before the crest we were greeted by a murderous fire. The Soviet artillery had zeroed in the road*

8ww2/2 Original caption: *Four kilometers before the capital city. The major (on the command wagon) is informed by civilians about the* *sition of Soviet troops.*

501ww2/2 Romanian soldiers receiving German decorations for bravery in action against the Soviets. The highly-mobile riflemen in this unit often made use of motorcycles or bicycles.

502ww2/2 Italian General Giovanni Messe inspecting *Bersaglieri*. In an attempt to show solidarity with Nazi Germany after Adolf Hitler attacked the Soviet Union, Mussolini created the *Corpo di Spedizione Italiano in Russia* (CSIR). Hitler showed little enthusiasm for this support. The CSIR was constituted on 10 July 1941 and, between July and August 1941, the units of the CSIR arrived in southern Russia.

03ww2/2 Major General Béla Miklós was the first commander of the Hungarian *Gyorshadtest* (Rapid Corps). This army consisted of two motorised brigades and a cavalry brigade, fighting with German Army Group South under von Rundstedt.

506ww2/2 *Generaloberst* Carl-Heinrich von Stülpnagel, commander of the German Seventeenth Army. Axis forces of Hungary and Slovakia operated in conjunction with eleven German divisions of the Seventeenth Army, Army Group South, under von Rundstedt.

Ferdinand Čatloš, commander of *Field Army Bernolák*, the army of the Axis Slovak Republic. It consisted of three infantry divisions and a 'Fast Troops Group', fighting with German Army Group South under von Rundstedt.

04ww2/2 *Feldmarschall* Gerd von Rundstedt, Commander-in-Chief of Army Group South, hosts Italian dictator, Benito Mussolini, and the German Führer, Adolf Hitler, on the Eastern Front in the late summer of 1941.

A German pontoon bridge, over the Dnieper near Kiev, thrown across the river in twenty-four hours, September 1941.

369ww2/2 A mechanized unit of Army Group South rests at Stariza, 21 November 1941, recently evacuated by the Russians, before continuing the fight east of Kiev.

59ww2/2 A Stug III Assault gun (*Gepanzerte Selbstfahrlafette für Sturmgeschütz 75 mm Kanone*) with crew, traversing marshes near the village f Berezhok, in southwest Ukraine, 14 August 1941.

62ww2/2 Hordes of Soviet prisoners were marched westward as September ended and October brought a worsening in the weather. Hitler's eemingly invincible warriors were about to experience a Russian winter.

448ww2/2 A German sentinel in the citadel of Kiev on 19 September 1941.

510ww2/2 On the cover of this glossy, illustrated German magazine, *Signal,* published by the *Wehrmacht,* a German army chaplain is depicted as caring for the spiritual well being of Russian peasants in conquered territories. The truth was very different. *Signal* was a propaganda tool, meant specifically for audiences in neutral, allied and occupied countries. A German edition was distributed in Switzerland, Axis countries and Nazi-occupied Europe. It was published fortnightly in twenty-five editions and thirty languages. At its height *Signal* had a circulation of 2,500,000 copies. The cover shown is the Dutch edition, dated 2 September 1941,

Returning to the faith. *Peasant women from the ravaged Ukraine have their children baptized by a chaplain of the German army.*

62ww2/2 Britain was dependent on imported goods and required more than a million tons of material every week to be able to survive and fight.

Chapter Seven: **Hitler Targets Britain's Atlantic Supplies**

60ww2/2 *Korvettenkapitän* Otto Kretschmer at his navigation periscope during a November 1940 patrol, for which he was awarded the Oak Leaves honour from Hitler. The patrol saw his U-99 sink three British armed merchant cruisers: HMS *Laurentic*, HMS *Patroclus* and HMS *Forfar*.

The Battle of the Atlantic was the longest military campaign of the Second World War, beginning in 1939 and continuing to the defeat of Nazi Germany in 1945. It centred on the Allied naval blockade of Germany, announced the day after the declaration of war and Germany' counter-blockade. The battle was at its peak from the summer of 1940 through to the winter of 1943. The Battle of the Atlantic pitted U-Boats and other warships of the *Kriegsmarine* and aircraft of the *Luftwaffe* against Allied merchant shipping carrying essential supplies to Britain. Escort vessels of the Royal Navy and, after Pearl Harbor, the United States Navy, became increasingly involved in employing new methods against U-Boats as the Allies fought to protect the vital cargoes.

677ww2/2 Admiral Dönitz and his staff plotting their next move in the bid to bring Britain to its knees, causing Churchill to seek a negotiated peace with Nazi German

679ww2/2 An Allied merchant ship in heavy seas, one vessel in a protective convoy, making the perilous voyage across the Atlantic.

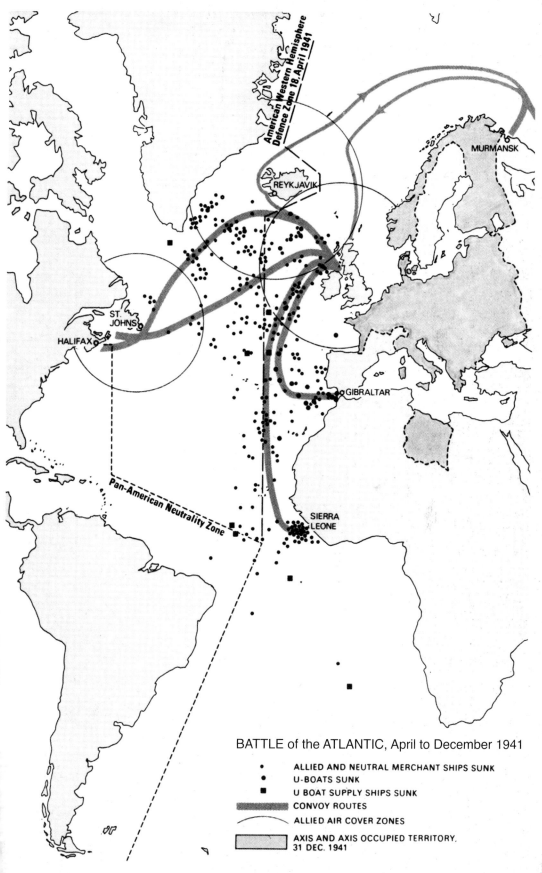

BATTLE of the ATLANTIC, April to December 1941

•   ALLIED AND NEUTRAL MERCHANT SHIPS SUNK
•   U-BOATS SUNK
■   U BOAT SUPPLY SHIPS SUNK

CONVOY ROUTES

ALLIED AIR COVER ZONES

AXIS AND AXIS OCCUPIED TERRITORY,
31 DEC. 1941

Labels on map: American Western Hemisphere Defence Zone 18. April 1941 · REYKJAVIK · MURMANSK · ST. JOHNS · HALIFAX · GIBRALTAR · Pan-American Neutrality Zone · SIERRA LEONE

656ww2/2 Officers on the bridge of a destroyer, escorting a large convoy of ships, keep a sharp look out for attacking enemy submarines during the Battle of the Atlantic, October 1941.

692ww2/2, 693ww2/2. Western Approaches Command HQ at Derby House, Liverpool. Commander RDS Crosse, Staff Officer Convoys, (left) discussing a special convoy movement map with Captain Lake, RN, Duty Officer. Operations room at the Canadian side of the Atlantic: The RCN-RCAF combined operations room at St. John's, Newfoundland and Labrador.

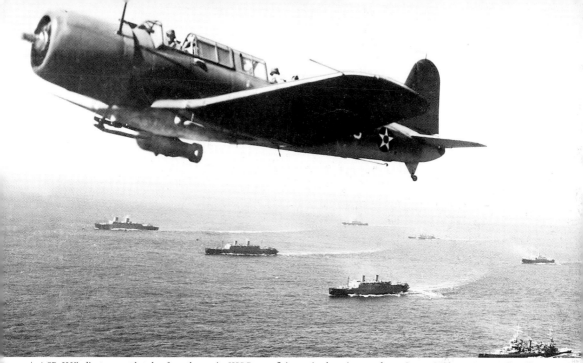

57ww2/2 A SB2U Vindicator scout bomber from the carrier USS Ranger flying anti-submarine patrol over Convoy WS-12, en route to Cape Town, November, 1941. The convoy was one of many escorted by the US Navy on 'Neutrality Patrol', before the United States officially entered the war in December 1941 after Pearl Harbor and Hitler's war declaration.

39ww2/2 A 210 Squadron Sunderland escorting convoy TC.6, 31 July 1940. Operating out of RAF Oban, a base located at the northern end of the Island of Kerrera, in Ardantrive Bay, west of Oban, Argyll and Bute, Scotland.

746ww2/2 The *Kriegsmarine* heavy cruiser *Admiral Scheer* with six 11 in guns in two triple turrets. Top speed of 32 mph left few battleships in the Anglo-French navies both able to catch her and powerful enough to sink her.

The KING has been graciously pleased to approve the award of the Victoria Cross to the late Commander (acting Captain) Edward Stephen Fogarty Fegen, Royal Navy. For valour in challenging hopeless odds and giving his life to save the many ships it was his duty to protect.

On the 5th of November, 1940, in heavy seas, Captain Fegen, in His Majesty's Armed Merchant Cruiser Jervis Bay, *was escorting thirty-eight Merchantmen. Sighting a powerful German warship he at once drew clear of the Convoy, made straight for the Enemy, and brought his ship between the Raider and her prey, so that they might scatter and escape. Crippled, in flames, unable to reply, for nearly an hour the* Jervis Bay *held the German's fire. So she went down but of the Merchantmen all but four or five were saved.*

747ww2/2 Admiral Theodor Krancke, captain of the *Admiral Scheer*. During the five month raiding cruise, the *Admiral Scheer* sank thirteen merchant ships, one armed merchant cruiser, HMS *Jervis Bay*, and captured three merchant ships, representing 115,195 tons of Allied and neutral shipping.

748ww2/2 HMS *Jervis Bay*.

Commander
Edward Stephen
Fogarty Fegen VC,
Royal Navy,
captain of HMS
Jervis Bay.

Jervis Bay's complement 255 officers and men; casualties 190; survivors sixty-five
Gallantry Awards

Midshipman Ronald Butler, RNR
Action Station – Aft Gun Control
Distinguished Service Cross
'One of the last to join the raft having been in the water for some time. He immediately took charge and showed outstanding leadership and initiative.'

Lieutenant Norman Wood, RNR
Distinguished Service Order
'As the senior surviving officer, I was impressed by his modesty and by the manner in which he took charge of the survivors in the Stureholm and since arrival at Halifax.'

Stoker George Beaman, RCNR
Action Station - Firefighting duties
Distinguished Service Medal
'Did excellent work in getting the rafts out and later on dived into the water several times in attempts to rescue men.'

Seaman Donald Bain, RNR
Action Station - AA gun-crew
Distinguished Service Medal
'He was extensively burnt endeavouring to save one of the same gun's crew who was on fire. He had previously been wounded on the scalp.'

Assist Steward William Barnett, MN
Action Station - Magazine room
Distinguished Service Medal
'Stationed in the foremost shell room when things went wrong and the lights went out. Barnett stuck to his post, endeavouring to get the emergency lighting to work. He would not leave his post until receiving orders to do so.'

Petty Officer Charles Castle
Action Station - Generating Room.
Distinguished Service Medal
'He displayed marked courage and leadership both during the action and later on after the ship had been abandoned. His example under most trying circumstances was a great help.'

ABS William Albert Cooper RNVR
Action Station - Sightsetter.
Distinguished Service Medal
'He was sightsetter on P1 gun. Orders had been given to abandon the forecastle and all men had left except Cooper. He had received no orders through his earphones and remained at his post. He stayed until he realised that the fore part of the ship had been abandoned. Only then did he leave.'

Stoker Dennis Drury MN
Distinguished Service Medal
'He took a prominent part in organising the launching of the rafts. The ship was being heavily shelled and Drury's coolness and determination were an example to everyone.'

ABS John Eggleston RFR
Action Station - Chief Gunner
Distinguished Service Medal
'He was No.1 on P2 gun. Although he was wounded he remained at his post and, by his example, kept the surviving members of the gun's crew together.'

Leading Seaman James Wood RNR
Conspicuous Gallantry Medal
'He showed outstanding leadership and initiative on the raft after the ship was abandoned. He gave everyone confidence and encouragement and concealed the fact that he was wounded in both thighs'.

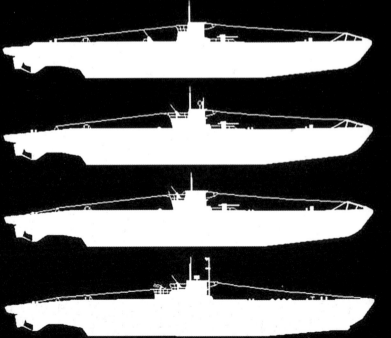

Type VII A

Type VII B

Type VII C

Type VII C/42

Kapitänleutnant Heinrich Lehmann-Willenbrock was sixth among the top twelve successful U-boat commanders during the Battle of the Atlantic against the Allies, in terms of tonnage of merchant ships sunk. He commanded four U-Boats and his most successful tour was commanding the U-*96,* a Type VIIC U-boat, which gained widespread recognition when one of its patrols was documented and publicized by an accompanying member of a propaganda company. The acclaimed *Das Boot* (1981), a German film and later TV series, was based upon this operational history.

684ww2/2 *Kapitänleutnant* Heinrich Lehmann-Willenbrock

683ww2/2 The submarine U-*96* in the Atlantic in 1941. The Type VIIC submarine had a maximum surface speed of 17.7 knots (20.4 mph) and a maximum submerged speed of 7.6 knots (8.7 mph). When submerged, the boat could operate for ninety-two miles at 4 knots (4.6 mph); when surfaced, she could travel 9,800 miles at 10 knots (12 mph). The U-*96* was fitted with five 21-inch torpedo tubes (four tubes at the bow and one at the stern). She carried fourteen torpedoes. One deck gun, an 88 mm SK C/35 with 220 rounds; for defence an anti-aircraft gun. The boat had a complement of between forty-four and sixty men.

682ww2/2 As part of *7.Unterseebootsflottille* (7th U-boat Flotilla), stationed in Saint Nazaire, on the French Atlantic coast, U-96 conducted eleven patrols, sinking twenty-seven ships. Seen here returning to Saint Nazaire in 1940, after a successful patrol, *Kapitänleutnant* Heinrich Lehmann-Willenbrock is facing the camera.

694ww2/2 One of the last Type VIIB boats to be built, *U-101* comes alongside the depot ship during her return journey to port.

695ww2/2, 696ww2/2 Torpedoes being loaded with care into the bow of U-48. A torpedo is protruding from one of the forward firing tubes and is being worked on in the confined space, which also served as sleeping quarters for the crew.

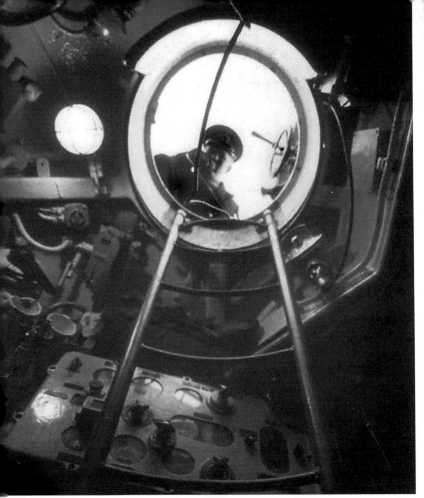

690ww2/2 Ladder inside the conning tower leading to the nerve centre of the submarine.

716ww2/2 Communications with base was through the Enigma coding machine, worked by the U-boat radio operator.

6ww2/2 Living conditions were cramped and rough, as space was at a premium; spaces had to double up as food storage areas, and for sleeping d relaxation.

1ww2/2 U-94, *Kapitänleutnant* Herbert Kuppisch, June 1941. He was a recipient of the Knight's Cross of the Iron Cross. Kuppisch and the crew U-847 were killed by aircraft from the US escort carrier USS *Card* on 27 August 1943. He was aged thirty-three.

706ww2/2 Oil soaked surviving crew members of a torpedoed merchantman being rescued..

707ww2/2 Victor and victim as seen from the conning tower of U-57. The ship sinking stern first is either the Norwegian tanker *Koll* or the British merchantman *Umtata*.

697ww2/2 Late on the afternoon of 27 April 1941, *Kapitänleutnant* Erich Topp in *U-522* came upon a big target: the 10,160 ton British freighter *Beacon Grange*, sailing alone, out of the Tyne en route for Buenos Aires loaded with ballast. Topp attacked submerged, firing all four bow tubes. The *Beacon Grange* crew radioed the submarine alert, 'SSS', then took to the lifeboats. Two days later the captain, seventy-three crew members and eight gunners were picked up by the Belgian trawler *Edouvard Anseele*; forty-one of the crew were transferred to HMS *Gladiolus* (K 34) and landed at Londonderry. Two crew members lost their lives from a complement of eighty-two.

708ww2/2 Survivors jump for safety to the steel deck of a U-boat.

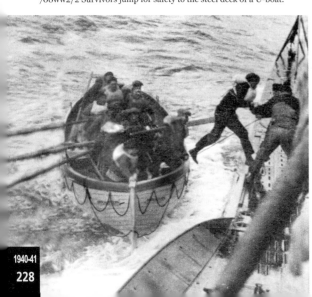

Capture of U-*110*, the Enigma encrypting machine and code books

SS *Athenia*

The SS *Athenia* was the first ship belonging to the Briish Empire to be sunk by Germany during the Second World War; sunk by U-*30*, commanded by Fritz-Julius Lemp on the day Britain declared war, 3 September 1939. One hundred and seventeen civilian passengers and crew were killed. The sinking was internationally condemned as a war crime. The dead included twenty-eight American citizens, leading Germany to fear that the US might react by joining the war on the side of Britain and France. The Nazi authorities denied that one of their submarines had sunk the ship. A German admission of responsibility did not come until the Nuremberg Trials in 1946.

Oberleutnant Fritz-Julius Lemp, seen here talking to Admiral Dönitz, claimed that the *Athenia* was a darkened ship steering a zigzag course, which seemed to be well off the normal shipping routes. This made him believe she was either a troopship, a Q-ship or an armed merchant cruiser. His ship's log book was altered to hide the crime and his crew was sworn to secrecy. The Germans claimed that Churchill was responsible for the sinking so as to bring the United States into the war on the side of the Allies.

In May 1941 Lemp was commanding U-*110* in the North Atlantic.

U-*110* had left Lorient on 15 April 1941. Twelve days later she sank the *Henri Mory* about 380 miles northwest of Ireland. Her next target was merchantmen of convoy OB 318 east of Greenland. She sank the *Esmond* and *Bengore Head*. Immediately the escort vessels, a corvette and two destroyers, counter-attacked. The British corvette, HMS *Aubrietia*, located the U-boat with sonar. *Aubrietia* and the destroyer HMS *Broadway*, dropped depth charges, forcing U-*110* to surface. As the crew turned out onto the U-boat's deck they came under fire from *Bulldog* and *Broadway*, inflicting casualties from gunfire and drowning. Lemp realised that U-*110* was not sinking and attempted to swim back to destroy the secret material. He was picked off in the water by a seaman. Including Lemp, fifteen men were killed in the action and thirty-two were captured. *Bulldog's* boarding party, led by Sub-Lieutenant David Balme, rescued her code book and Enigma machine. U-*110* was taken in tow but sank en route to Scapa Flow.

Commander Joe Baker-Cresswell, was commanding convoy OB 318's escort group. His flag ship was the *Bulldog*.

HMS *Broadway*

HMS *Aubrietia*

HMS *Bulldog*

HMS *Bulldog* with U-*110* in tow

717ww2/2 The quarterdeck lookout on board HMS *Viscount* is searching the sea for any tell-tale signs of a periscope cutting the waves, indicating the presence of a stalking U-Boat. He is leaning against a Thornycroft Mark II depth charge thrower.

718ww2/2 After a U-Boat hunt in the Atlantic, sailors are placing a depth charge into position in a depth charge rack for dropping from the stern of the destroyer HMS *Eskimo*. Although a depth charge attack could be nerve-wracking to a U-boat crew, the pressure hull would not rupture unless the charge detonated closer than approximately 15 feet. Placing the charge within this range was a matter of chance. Most U-boats sunk by depth charges were destroyed by damage accumulated during a long barrage rather than a single charge.

719ww2/2 Rolling depth charges from the stern of a United States Navy destroyer defending 'neutral' merchant ships in the Atlantic.

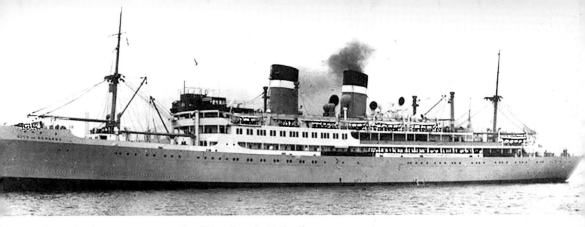

711ww2/2 The SS *City of Benares*.

713ww2/2 A lifeboat from the SS *City of Benares* is finally rescued after eight days on the waves of the Atlantic. This boat had five children on board.

Convoy OB-213, comprising twenty ships, left Liverpool for Quebec and Montreal on 13 September, 1940; SS *City of Benares* was flagship of the convoy for commodore Rear Admiral E.J.G. Mackinnon and the first ship in the centre column. Just before midnight on 17 September, the *City of Benares* was targeted by *U-48*, commanded by *Kapitänleutnant* Heinrich Bleichrodt. After missing with two torpedoes he launched a third and struck her in the stern, causing her to sink within thirty minutes. The *Benares* was being used as an evacuee ship and was transporting ninety children passengers from wartime blitzed Britain to Canada and safety. Of the 407 people on board, 260 lost their lives; of these seventy-seven were children with ages ranging from six to fifteen. There were just thirteen survivors out of the original ninety evacuees. The sinking caused public outrage in Britain, leading to Winston Churchill cancelling the Children's Overseas Reception Board (CORB) plan to relocate British children abroad. The Germans defended the attack as being made on a legitimate target, insisting that the British government was to blame for allowing children to travel in war zones when the German government had issued repeated warnings. Crew members of *U-48*, later expressed their regret once it became known that the ship they had sunk had been carrying children. They reaffirmed that there was no way that they could have known who was on board.

714ww2/2 *U-48* coming into Kiel. During her career she carried out twelve patrols and sank fifty-nine ships. She was decommissioned on 25 September 1943 and used for training purposes.

Kapitänleutnant Heinrich Bleichrodt, commander of *U-48*, September 1940.

720ww2/2, 727ww2/2 An RAF Hudson; cockpit and crew detail. A Hudson of No 269 Squadron, piloted by Squadron Leader James Thompson, dropped its four 250-pound depth charges; one detonated just ten yards from the boat, which knocked out all electrical power, smashed instruments, caused water leaks and contaminated the air on the boat. The inexperienced crew believed the contamination to be chlorine gas and panicked. The Hudson fired on them, but stopped when the U-Boat crew displayed a white sheet.

In April 1941 RAF Squadron No 269 was moved to Iceland, where it flew medium range anti-submarine patrols, helping to fill the mid-Atlantic aerial protection gap, as well as flying cover for convoys to Russia. On 27 August 1941, the squadron was involved in an unusual action. Submarine U-570 was caught on the surface; it dived but was damaged by depth charges and forced to the top. It was the U-Boat's maiden voyage and the inexperienced crew became unnerved by the loss of electrical services and leakage of what they thought to be chlorine gas and opted to surrender. The U-Boat was escorted into port and later was commissioned into the Royal Navy as HMS *Graph*.

722ww2/2 The U-570, a brand new Type VIIC submarine, with her conning tower packed with her crew waiting for a ship to arrive to take them prisoner. They have been warned that any attempt to scuttle the vessel would result in them being machine gunned. Note that the fore and aft hatches are open.

728ww2/2 The Royal Navy enjoying their prize capture – giving the thumbs up..

23ww2/2 The German submarine U-570 enters dock at Barrow-in-Furness after her capture by the Royal Navy. She provided both the Royal Navy and United States Navy with significant information on German submarines and carried out three combat patrols with a Royal Navy crew.

4ww2/2 A Royal Navy sub-lieutenant working the chart-table in the control room of HMS Graph, the former U-570, February 1942.

725ww2/2 Some of the Royal Navy crew of HMS Graph, the former U-570, having supper in the forward torpedo room during sea-trials, February 1942.

5ww2/2 HMS Graph, the former U-570, at Holy Loch, Scotland, after she had ceased active service and been reassigned for training, April 1943.

1940-41

721ww2/2 Squadron Leader James Thompson: *We owe the Navy a personal word of thanks. They came down to our station and handed over to the squadron a wonderful memento of the occasion, a memento of which we shall always be very proud – the U-boat's flag.* (The flag from U-570 is now kept by the RAF Museum, Hendon.)

During the Second World War, RAF personnel regularly described their experiences on the radio for listeners of the BBC. One man was Pilot Officer Ron Down of No 233 Squadron. On 23 July 1941, Pilot Officer Down took off from RAF Aldergrove at the controls of a Lockheed Hudson. In his own words he related what happened.

At 08:01 on 23 July 1941, just as Pilot Officer Ron Down's Hudson was about to leave a convoy, an escorting corvette flashed a message: *Suspicious aircraft to starboard!* This is Down's description of the action that followed:

"We sighted an aircraft about four miles away. It was flying very low, just above the sea, and on a steady course towards the convoy, taking good advantage of the very low cloud over the Atlantic. It was just a dot at first – but obviously a big fellow. I went on to have a look at him. Just as a precaution, I pulled down my front gun sights, and mentioned to my co-pilot [Pilot Officer Corken] that I had 'the stranger' beautifully in my sights.

"He suddenly let out an Irish yell. 'It's a bloody Condor!' he cried. He was jolly well right, too. It was a Focke-Wulf Condor, painted sea-green as camouflage. The big German was going straight for the convoy and was now only two miles from it.

"The second pilot ran back to man the side gun of the Hudson. I went all out on the throttle and at 1,100 feet began to dive. Four hundred yards away I was wondering who would fire first. At that moment the German and I began firing simultaneously, but my front guns didn't seem to be doing him any damage.

"The enemy's shooting was bad. Not one of his bullets or cannon shells hit us then, or afterwards. I brought my Hudson still lower and got into position 200 yards away to give my rear gunner a chance. He took it beautifully and promptly. I could see the tracer bullets from his tail gun whipping into the Focke-Wulf's two port engines and into its fuselage. We got closer still – actually to

715ww2/2 A Fw 200 Condor from *Kampfgeschwader* (KG) 40 patroling over the Atlantic.

between 20-30 feet – so close that the Focke-Wulf looked like house. All the time my tail-gunner's tracers were still ripping in the Jerry. When there was only eight yards between us we saw gun poked out from a window of the Focke-Wulf. A face appeare above it, but it wasn't there long. The second pilot saw the fac and spoiled it with a burst from his side guns.

"By this time two of the four engines of the Focke-Wulf we aglow. The German turned. As he did so he showed us his bel My tail and side guns absolutely raked it. I made a tight turn th other way. When the Hudson came out of it, I saw the Germa about a mile away still flying apparently all right. We know th these big Focke-Wulfs are built to take heavy punishment. Bu was amazed this fellow could still fly at all after the hiding we h given him. I set off after him again, but the chase didn't last lor The Focke-Wulf soon crashed into the sea. It pancaked on t water, and we could see five members of its crew swimming fro the wreckage and another one scampering along the fuselag

We went round them a few times until saw the six survivors hanging on to a rubb dinghy. The last we heard was that th were picked up by one of our warships.

"We had a last look at the convoy. Eve man on board the warships and merche vessels, from captains to cooks, seemed be on deck, waving and signalling th thanks for the grandstand view of the enc another Focke-Wulf. My relief was now sight and so I made for home."

688ww2/2 A four-engined Fw 200 flying low over an Atlantic convoy just after dropping its bombs.

87ww2/2 The Focke Wulf Condor being abandoned by its crew after being shot down by Hudson AM536 of No 233 Squadron, out of Aldergrove, 3 July 1941. The Condor had been shadowing a west bound convoy. Six of the Luftwaffe crew were picked up by a Royal Navy escort vessel. Photographed from Down's Hudson: the crew of F8+BB struggle to climb into their dinghy, which is inflating to the right of the tailplane.

686ww2/2 Condors of *Stab 1./KG40* at Bordeaux-Merignac, France, being prepared for operations. Likely the aircraft here is F8+BB – the same aircraft shot down by Pilot Officer Down and his crew. The German crew who were captured consisted of *Oberfeldwebel* Heinrich Bleichert, the pilot who maanaged to ditch, allowing the other crew members – *Oberfeldwebel* Josef Raczak, *Feldwebel* Karl Uebelhofer, *Gefreiter* Josef Weid, *Oberfeldwebel* Heinrich Grube, and *Obergefreiter* Anton Rogenhofer – to abandon the plane and reach their dingy. The sole fatal casualty was a civilian meteorologist named August Dollinger.

To counter the threat of the Condor the Admiralty developed the fighter catapult ship – a converted freighter, manned by a naval crew, carrying a single Hawker Hurricane fighter. When an enemy bomber was sighted, the fighter would be launched into the air and climb to intercept the bomber. Being large and slow, the Fw 200 was an easy target. After combat, the Hurricane pilot would ba out or ditch in the ocean near the convoy; then be picked up, if all went well. The CAM ships were a stop-gap solution until sufficier. Royal Navy escort carriers became available. The CAM ship was equipped with a rocket-propelled catapult, launching a single Hawker Hurricane, dubbed a 'Hurricat' or 'Catafighter'.

729ww2/2 Test launch of a Hurricane at Greenock, Scotland, from a CAM, 31 May 1941. The first RAF trial CAM launch was from SS *Empire Rainbow* at Greenock on the River Clyde on 31 May 1941

30ww2/2 A Royal Air Force Hawker Hurricane Mk IA on the catapult of a CAM (Catapult Armed Merchant) ship at Greenock, Scotland.

31ww2/2 Flight Lieutenant Douglas Richard Turley-George and spare pilot Flying Officer C Fenwick with their Hurricane aboard SS *Empire Tide*. The merchantmen CAMs, were allocated fifty Hawker Hurricane fighters with specially trained RAF crews. In spite of heavy losses and the one-flight-only waste of aircraft, the catapult ships remained in service until 1943.

732ww2/2 Pilot Officer Alistair Hay, Royal Air Force Volunteer Reserve. A Hurricane catapult pilot from South Africa.

733ww2/2 The CAM, *Empire Lawrence*, on 27 May 1942, the ship forming part of the PQ16 convoy to Murmansk. Pilot Officer Hay was serving as a Catapult Pilot aboard this vessel when the convoy was attacked by six Heinkels. Hay's mission was to disrupt the torpedo bombing runs and destroy as many enemy aircraft as possible. He diverted the attack and in the process destroyed one aircraft and damaged a second. He was wounded in the action, shot in the thigh and, bleeding heavily, he had to bale out of his aircraft. The rescue was also dramatic as HMS *Volunteer* also came under attack as they were hoisting Alistair Hay aboard and HMS *Volunteer* had to make some dramatic evasive manoeuvres.

For his actions Pilot Officer Alistair Hay was subsequently awarded the Distinguished Flying Cross (DFC); his citation reads:

Pilot Officer Hay was pilot of the Hurricane on board a ship fitted with a catapult. On the approach of enemy aircraft he was catapulted off and immediately proceeded to attack and drive off a formation of six Heinkel 111's and 115's which were preparing to deliver a torpedo attack on the port bow of the convoy; not only did this prevent synchronisation with an attack which developed from the starboard bow, but he destroyed one Heinkel 111 and slightly damaged another. Pilot Officer Hay was himself wounded and he then baled out and was picked up by one of His Majesty's ships of the convoy escort. He showed great gallantry and his spirited attack was a great encouragement to all the convoy and escorts, and cannot but have been a great discomfort and surprise to the enemy.

Waiting for the Condors – pilot Tim Elkington poses with his whistle in his teeth.

Based on the memories and log book of a CAM (Catapult Aircraft Merchant ships) pilot, Tim Elkington.

In 1941-2 Tim was involved in a ferry operation; a detachment of his squadron was delivering Hurricane IIBs to Vaenga, in Northern Russia. He had returned to Northern Ireland, where he was enjoying converting to Spitfire VBs. He mentions how his euphoria was spoiled when he received a posting to MSFU, Merchant Ship Fighter Unit, RAF Speke, Liverpool, which provided pilots for the CAM Ships. Requirements for pilots engaged in this dangerous assignment were set out, in part, as follows:

It is of paramount importance that pilots in the MSFU must be first class men in combat, because they operate on their own and, on them and them alone, may depend the safety of many hundreds of thousands of tons of merchant shipping and cargo which form the life line of this country. They must be reliable and keen, have tact and initiative, and be able to engage the enemy after long periods of inactivity. They must also be good sailors.

Any launch had to end in a ditching or bale-out and it was our hope that some unit of the escort force would be able to disengage for long enough to pull us out of the ocean. This they achieved with aplomb, the slowest rescue taking seven minutes.

I was very grateful for a posting back to my old squadron, No 1 Squadron [converting to Typhoons at Acklington, July 1942], shortly before I was due to sail on the fateful PQ 17 convoy to Russia.

35ww2/2 The German auxiliary cruiser, KMS *Thor*, in the South Atlantic, 1940. Requisitioned as a commerce raider; armed, equipped and put into service in March 1940. Very fast for a cargo ship. Its 150 mm guns came from the old battleship *Deutschland*. The raider, known by British intelligence as **Raider E**, sank or captured twelve ships on her first trip, ten more on the second.

742ww2/2 *Kapitän zur See* Otto Kähler, captain of the *Thor*.

Nazi commerce raiders: Germany sent out two waves of six surface raiders each during the early years of the Second World War. Many of these vessels had originally been refrigerator ships, used to transport fresh food from the tropics. They were faster than most merchant vessels; this was important for their commerce raider role. Most were armed with: six 5.9 inch guns; various smaller guns; torpedoes; reconnaissance seaplanes; and some were equipped for minelaying. Several captains demonstrated great creativity in disguising their vessels to masquerade as Allied or as neutral merchant ships.

The German auxiliary cruiser *Atlantis* was sunk on 22 November 1941 by the British cruiser HMS *Devonshire*. Salvos hit *Atlantis*, killing seven sailors as the crew abandoned ship; her captain, Bernhard Rogge, was the last off. Ammunition exploded, the bow rose into the air, and the ship sank. After the *Devonshire* had left, U-*126* surfaced and picked up 300 German sailors and a wounded American prisoner. The submarine carried and towed rafts towards Brazil and safety.

Observation on the conduct of *Kapitän zur See* Bernhard Rogge:

His treatment of prisoners left respect, instead of hatred.

Captain J. Armstrong White, of the British ship, *City of Baghdad*, sunk by the *Atlantis*, July 1941.

9ww2/2, 741ww2/2. The German commerce raider *Atlantis* **Raider C**. *Kapitän zur See* Bernhard Rogge, captain of the *Atlantis*, had been forced to apply for a 'German Blood Certificate', that would allow his racial background to be overlooked – (as he had a Jewish grandparent).

737ww2/2 *Pinguin* (**Raider F** to the British Admiralty) was the first of the *Kriegsmarine's* auxiliary cruisers to be sunk. She had sailed over 59,000 miles in 357 days at sea. She sank or captured twenty-eight ships; some captured vessels were sent back to Germany under prize crews. Four more ships were sunk by mines sewn by *Pinguin*.

Pinguin had been targeting shipping routes between the Persian Gulf and Mozambique. On 8 May 1941, her lookouts spotted the silhouette of a British warship on the horizon and altered course away from it at maximum speed. It was the British cruiser HMS *Cornwall*, searching for the commerce raider. The *Cornwall* launched a Supermarine Walrus aircraft, which spotted the disguised *Pinguin* flying the Norwegian ensign and displaying the name *Tamerlane* on the sides of her bridge. *Tamerlane* was not among the names on the list of merchant ships known to be in the area at that time. *Cornwall* radioed to the circling Walrus to inform the 'Norwegians' that the ship bearing down on them was British and to order them to heave to. *Pinguin* adopted the classic defensive response of presenting her stern. Warning shots were fired and a second Walrus was prepared for launching, armed with two 250-pound bombs. It was ordered to drop the first bomb in front of the fleeing *Pinguin* and if that failed to halt her the second bomb was to be dropped on her forecastle. *Pinguin*, dropped her disguise, ran up her battle flag, turned sharply to port to bring her full broadside to bear and opened up with five guns simultaneously, straddling *Cornwall*. *Cornwall* suffered a failure in the electrical circuit that controlled the training of her main gun turrets. She broke off and retired out of range of *Pinguin's* guns to carry out repairs. Out of range of *Pinguin's*

736ww2/2 *Kapitän zur See* Ernst Felix Krüder, captain of the *Pinguin*.

guns, the damage to her turret circuits on Cornwall was repaired. The first Walrus was spotting for the *Cornwall's* gunners, who began to register her first hits, bringing down the foremast. Krüder gave the orders to release the prisoners and to set the scuttling charges and abandon ship. At that very moment a four-gun salvo from the *Cornwall's* 8-inch forward turrets destroyed the raider. One shell struck the stored sea mines and *Penguin* blew apart.

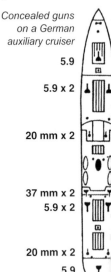

Concealed guns on a German auxiliary cruiser

5.9
5.9 x 2
20 mm x 2
37 mm x 2
5.9 x 2
20 mm x 2
5.9

743ww2/2 A ship launched Supermarine Walrus.

738ww2/2 HMS *Cornwall*. Of the 401 Germans aboard *Pinguin,* only three officers, one prize officer and 57 petty officers and men survived. Of the 238 prisoners, only nine officers and fifteen seamen survived. 214 prisoners and 341 of *Pinguin's* crew were killed.

759ww2/2 Marking up victory pennants showing the tonnage of shipping sunk. There was a tendency for U-Boat captains to exaggerate the size of their victims. Dönitz was aware of this as it created a problem when it came to estimating the shipping resources of the Allies.

2ww2/2 *Kapitänleutnant* Jürgen esten, commanding U-*106*. On her aiden patrol from Germany to her base Lorient, U-*106* sank two ships with a tal of 13,640 tons. *Kapitänleutnant* esten received his Knights Cross on her cond patrol in African waters, where he ık eight ships, totalling 44,820 tons.

oww2/2 Summer 1941, Type IXB U-6 coming into Lorient with pennants licating 59,000 tons sunk. Oesten is ecting the berthing.

1ww2/2 German nurses bearing uquets of flowers greeting U-106 at rient. The officers and crews were ated as heroes and decorations were arded, usually to the captains, at ckside celebrations. As the sea war ogressed these niceties dwindled as the Boat losses mounted.

So, for our naval warfare, we have secured the ports of the Bay of Biscay. I am most happy about that. At the beginning of the campaign I was determined to get the French Channel ports for our submarine warfare.
ADOLF HITLER

Korvettenkapitän Otto Kretschmer was responsible for the sinking of forty-seven vessels in the space of just eighteen months. His short but prolific spell with the *Kriegsmarine* U-Boat arm accounted for the sinking of 273,043 tons of shipping. This total was more than any other naval commander throughout the Second World War. His career was cut short when he was captured in March 1941. HMS *Walker* attacked his U-99 with depth charges as she defended convoy HX112. Serious damage was incurred and Kretschmer scuttled U-99 3.45 am on 17 March 1941. He and his crew were taken prisoner aboard the *Walker*.

That March two more aces were hunted and killed: Prien and U went down with all hands on 8 March. Schepke died on the same day that Kretschmer scuttled U In less than two weeks, three of Germany's ace U-boat commanders disappeared from serving officers' roll of Admiral Dönitz.

673ww2/2 At the Reichs Chancellery in Berlin Adolf Hitler presented the U-Boat Commander Otto Kretschmer with the Oak Leaves to the Knight's Cross of the Iron Cross, 13 November 1940.

Prien killed 8 March 1941

Schepke killed 17 March 19

Twelve of the top U-boat a **with over 155,000 tons** **shipping claimed destroy**

61ww2/2 Otto Kretschmer comes ashore at the Prince's Landing Stage in Liverpool and into captivity. His luck finally run out on 17 March, 1941, when HMS *Walker* an HMS *Vanoc* attacked his U-99 with depth charges as the defended a convoy.

Korvettenkapitän
Otto Ketschmer
47 ships sunk (273,043 tons)

Kapitänleutnant
Wolfgang Lüth
46 ships sunk (225,204 tons)

Kapitänleutnant
Erich Topp
35 ships sunk (197,460 tons)

Korvettenkapitän
Heinrich Liebe
34 ships sunk (187,267 tons)

Korvettenkapitän
Viktor Schütze
35 ships sunk (180,073 tons)

Kapitänleutnant
Heinrich Lehmann-Willenbrock
24 ships sunk (170,237 tons)

Korvettenkapitän
Karl-Friedrich Merten
26 ships sunk (170,151 tons)

Kapitänleutnant
Herbert Schultze
26 ships sunk (169,709 tons)

Kapitänleutnant
Günther Prien
30 ships sunk (162,769 tons)

Oberleutnant zur See
Georg Lassen
26 ships sunk (156,082 tons)

Kapitänleutnant
Joachim Schepke
37 ships sunk (tons 155,882)

Oberleutnant zur See
Werner Henke
24 sunk (155,714 tons)

Children rescued from
a liner torpedoed in
the Atlantic.

A U-Boat crew
celebrating Christmas
on Atlantic patrol.

54ww2-2 When Mussolini declared war on France and Britain on 10 June 1940, the following day Italian bombers took off from Sicily to bomb Malta. SM 79 bombers in formation; the most widely produced Italian bomber.

Chapter Eight: **The Axis Target Malta**

55ww2-2 A 40 mm Bofors anti-aircraft gun protecting the Grand Harbor at Valletta, Malta, 1940. The weapon is located in Upper Barrakka Gardens looking towards Fort St Michael. The siege of the British colony began in June 1940 and aerial attacks would last two and a half years.

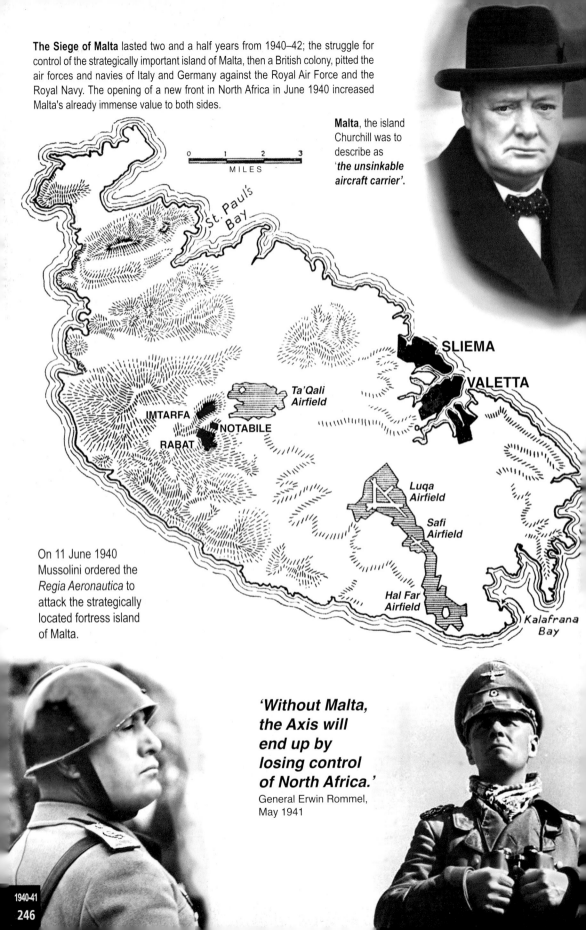

The Siege of Malta lasted two and a half years from 1940–42; the struggle for control of the strategically important island of Malta, then a British colony, pitted the air forces and navies of Italy and Germany against the Royal Air Force and the Royal Navy. The opening of a new front in North Africa in June 1940 increased Malta's already immense value to both sides.

Malta, the island Churchill was to describe as '*the unsinkable aircraft carrier'*.

0 1 2 3
MILES

St. Paul's Bay

SLIEMA

VALETTA

Ta'Qali Airfield

IMTARFA

NOTABILE

RABAT

Luqa Airfield

Safi Airfield

On 11 June 1940 Mussolini ordered the *Regia Aeronautica* to attack the strategically located fortress island of Malta.

Hal Far Airfield

Kalafrana Bay

'*Without Malta, the Axis will end up by losing control of North Africa.'*
General Erwin Rommel, May 1941

763ww2/2, 770ww2/2. Gloster Sea Gladiater Mk 1, *Faith,* of the trio *Faith, Hope* and *Charity* [Love], (from the Bible letter to the Corinthians: 1 Cor. 13:13). For several weeks in June 1940 the island of Malta was protected by a small force of biplane fighters, based at RAF Hal Far. A petrol bowser at Hal Far refueling the island's early defenders.

Mussolini resolved to bomb and starve Malta into submission: ports and towns, along with Allied shipping supplying the island, would be targeted. This resolve resulted in Malta becoming one of the most intensively bombed areas of the war. The *Regia Aeronautica* and the *Luftwaffe* flew a total of 3,000 bombing raids, dropping 6,700 tons of bombs on the Grand Harbour area alone, over a period of two years in an effort to destroy British defences and the ports. Success would have made possible a combined German–Italian amphibious landing, supported by German *Fallschirmjäger*. In the event, Allied convoys were able to supply and reinforce Malta, while the RAF defended its airspace – but at great cost.

773ww2/2 SM79 bombers on a mission. Thirty bombers of the *Regia Aeronautica* took off from Catania in Sicily heading for Malta and the airfield at Hal Far. A further flight of bombers was assigned to bomb the dockyards at Valletta and another ten bombers the seaplane base at Kalafrana – It was 11 June 1940. The radar station on Malta picked up the incoming raiders and the Gladiators at Hal Far took off to intercept them.

772ww2/2 The Grand Harbour, with fires burning in Valletta following a raid. A number of civilians and six bandsmen of the 1st Coast Regiment were killed. One Italian Macchi MC.200 Saetta escort fighter was claimed by Flying Officer Woods.

775ww2/2 Flying Officer William 'Timber' Woods.

776ww2/2 Flight Lieutenant George Burges.

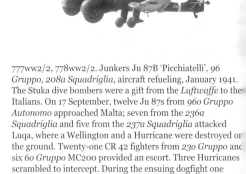

777ww2/2, 778ww2/2. Junkers Ju 87B 'Picchiatelli', 96 *Gruppo*, 208a *Squadriglia*, aircraft refueling, January 1941. The Stuka dive bombers were a gift from the *Luftwaffe* to the Italians. On 17 September, twelve Ju 87s from 960 *Gruppo Autonomo* approached Malta; seven from the 236a *Squadriglia* and five from the 237a *Squadriglia* attacked Luqa, where a Wellington and a Hurricane were destroyed on the ground. Twenty-one CR 42 fighters from 230 *Gruppo* and six 60 *Gruppo* MC200 provided an escort. Three Hurricanes scrambled to intercept. During the ensuing dogfight one Italian Ju 87 was claimed by Flying Officer 'Jock' Barber and Flying Officer Woods shot down a CR 42 from the 70a *Squadriglia*.

On 23 June 1940 there was a raid by bombers from *11 Stormo* with MC.200 fighters flying escort. Two Gladiators, flown by Timber Woods and George Burges, were scrambled. The Gladiators attacked the bombers (five S.79s escorted by three MC.200s) without obvious result. Burges was then attacked by one of the escorting fighters, an aircraft of *88a Squadriglia*. Burges took on the fighter and a dogfight ensued over the sea off Sliema. The faster Macchi had the initiative but kept overshooting the nimble Gladiator, allowing Burges to 'belt him up the backside as he went past'. After four or five such passes the Macchi suddenly caught fire and the pilot baled out over the sea.

774ww2/2 A Macchi MC.200 was faster than the Gladiators but not half as manouverable.

71ww2/2 Sir William Dobbie, acting Governor General, Malta. Forced into the role of Commander in Chief when General Sir Bonham-Carter was invalided back to England, April 1940.

779ww2/2, 783ww2/2, 784ww2/2. Vital supplies being unloaded on the quayside of the Grand Harbour, Malta. Convoys running the gauntlet of Mussolini's 'mare nostro' (his Mediterranean Sea).

82ww2/2 HMS *Illustrious* on convoy duty, providing air cover for ships bringing supplies to Malta.

786ww2/2 The first action by German bombers against Malta and Royal Navy convoys to sustain the island took place on 10 January 1941. Ju 88A bombers of *KG 54* of *Fliegerkorps X* take off from an airfield in Sicily. Their task was to maintain continuous attacks against the island.

780ww2/2, 785ww2/2, 781ww2/2 A near miss, HMS *Illustrious* attacked by dive bombers on 10 January 1941 in the Mediterranean off the Italian island of Pantelleria, in the first action by German bombers in the Mediterranean. HMS *Illustrious* survived a ferocious attack, including that of over forty Ju 87 Stukas and Ju 88 bombers, to make it to Malta for repairs. The aicraft carrier can be seen berthed at Parlatorio wharf listing to port, next to the large crane. Wave after wave of bombers – more than seventy, rained down bombs on the dockyard and area. The attacks killed 126 officers and men and wounded ninety-one.

787ww2/2 Taxiing for take-off, a Hurricane of No 261 Squadron at Ta Kali 1941. The RAF was in no condition to prevent a major German air attack, with just sixteen Hurricanes and a couple of serviceable Gladiators available.

788ww2/2 The Fairey Fulmar. Fulmars flying off the aircraft carrier *Illustrious* were the only effective fighter defence against the concentrated attacks of the *Luftwaffe* and the Italian Air Force.

789ww2/2 Without aircraft aboard, HMS *Illustrious* sailed to Alexandria on 23 January 1941 escorted by four destroyers, for temporary repairs that lasted until 10 March. From there she sailed through the Suez Canal, round Africa to America, where she received permanent repairs.

Lieutenant Commander Malcolm David Wanklyn and his entire crew were reported missing in action on 14 April 1942. Wanklyn was a Royal Navy submarine ace and one of the most successful submariners in the Allied navies. Wanklyn and his crew sank sixteen enemy vessels. These included two Italian submarines; a rare achievement.

791ww2/2 Lieutenant Commander Malcolm David Wanklyn VC, DSO with his first lieutenant, Lieutenant J R D Drummond, of HMS *Upholder*.

790ww2/2 Resupplying at Manoel Island Royal Navy submarine base.

792ww2/2 *Capitano di Fregata* Vittorio Moccagatta. Commander of the *X Light Flotilla* (a special forces branch of the Italian Navy).

At dawn on 26 July, 1941, the Italian Navy mounted a daring attempt to penetrate the Grand Harbour and Marsamxett Creek in this the first assault against Malta from the sea. The attack on Valletta began when the *X Flottiglia* craft sailed from its base at Augusta in Sicily, led by the sloop *Diana* – Mussolini's private yacht – which carried nine E-boats (called *barchini)* to a point twenty miles north of Malta. Accompanying her were two motor launches, one of these with the leader of the expedition, Capitano di Fregata Vittorio Moccagatta. Two human torpedoes, known as SLCs, were embarked on another launch.

The plan was for the two SLCs to enter Marsamxett and attack the British submarine base at Lazzaretto and for the *barchini* to force their way through the breakwater and sink ships in the Grand Harbour. The presence of the sloop *Diana* and her accompanying craft was picked up by radar at 10.30 pm. All coastal defences at Fort St Elmo and Fort Ricasoli were alerted. At 4.45 am the first *barchino* rammed the nets barring entrance to Grand Harbour. The explosive charges failed to explode, whereupon the pilot of a second craft decided to smash his *Siluro a Lenta Corsa* (SLC or slow-running torpedo) against the bridge, a manoeuvre he knew would lead to his death. When the vessel impacted with the pedestal of the bridge it set off explosives in the stationary first craft, demolishing one of the spans. The span fell astride the gap, which the Italians hoped would give them access into the harbour but, contrary to their plans, completely blocked the passage. The

793ww2/2 *Capitano di Corvette* Giorgio Giobbe commander of the surface division. He was killed when a Hurricane strafed his boat on the return trip to Sicily. To honor his memory he was awarded the Gold Medal for Military Valour.

explosion alerted the 6 pdr twin gun crews in the two harbour forts and within two minutes all the attacking craft were either sunk or disabled by the gunners of the Royal Malta Artillery. Only one launch managed to reach Sicily, with eleven men on board. Sixteen had lost their lives in the attack and eighteen were taken prisoner. The commander, Vittorio Moccagatta, was killed by the defensive fire from the forts.

794ww2/2 The blown-up bridge that blocked the intended channel for the MTMs.

796ww2/2 MAS 451 took part in the raid. It succeeded in bringing down a Hawker Hurricane before blowing it up.

795ww2/2 An MTM *barchini* at attack speed: the rudder set, the pilot is about to roll off. The boat is packed with explosives.

798ww2/2 The Italian human torpedo the *Siluro a Lenta Corsa* SLC.

797ww2/2 *Maggiore* (Major) Tesei was killed when he rode his torpedo into the bridge support at the harbour entrance at Malta. He was awarded the Gold Medal for Military Valour.

On the 7 June, 1941 Winston Churchill sent a telegram to Lieutenant General Dobbie pledging full support in the protection of Malta.

You may be sure we regard Malta as one of the master-keys of the British Empire. We are sure you are the man to hold it and we will do everything in human power to give you the means.

Reinforcements began to arrive at Malta.

800ww2/2 The Governor of Malta, Sir William Dobbie, and commander in chief 1941.

803ww2/2, 804ww2/2, 805ww2/2. Crew of a Vickers Mk VIb Light Tank servicing one of their Vickers machine guns in the field. The 'stone wall' paintwork was unique to Malta Command. British Infantry 3 inch mortars firing during an exercise. Helmets are painted in Malta rock camouflage. A Bren gun carrier is used to tow a trolley of 250 lb bombs to a Vickers Wellington Mk II at RAF Luqa.

RAF Bomber squadrons based on the 'unsinkable aircraft carrier Malta' played two important roles: direct attacks on Axis positions and supply dumps in the Western Desert and attacks on the Axis supply route across the Mediterranean. To eliminate the threat played by the island fortress, with its airfields and deep habours, the intense bombing of Malta by the *Luftwaffe* and the *Regia Aeronautica* was set to continue and increase in ferocity in the third year of the Second World War.

799ww2/2 A squadron of Wellington bombers during a dusk operation on Sicily 1941.

02ww2 The British Expeditionary Force had been severely beaten and evacuated at Dunkirk; a recruiting and training programme was set in motion to provide the British Empire with the manpower to hit back. A special pro-active force was born to deliver strikes against the Third Reich.

Chapter Nine: Churchill Sets Europe Ablaze

08ww2 Operation Claymore was a British commando raid on the Norwegian Lofoten Islands. The islands were an important centre for the production of fish oil and glycerine, used in the German war economy.

Enterprises must be prepared, with specially trained troops of the hunter class, who can develop a reign of terror down these coasts, first of all on the 'butcher and bolt' policy.

Winston Churchill,
6 June 1940

The Chief of the Imperial General Staff at that time was General Sir John Dill, his military assistant was Lieutenant Colonel Dudley Clarke. Clarke discussed the matter with Dill at the War Office and was asked to prepare a paper on the subject. Clarke proposed the formation of a new force based on tactics adopted by the Boer commandos in the South African Wars around the turn of the century: *'hit sharp and quick – then run to fight another day'*. Dill, aware of Churchill's mind set, approved Clarke's proposal. From then onwards the special force became **The Commandos**.

809ww2/2, 810ww2/2 General Sir John Dill; Lieutenant Colonel Dudley Clarke.

For Operation Collar the Royal Air Force was approached for the use of four of its air sea rescue boats based at Dover, Ramsgate and Newhaven to transport the commandos on their first raid.

Following the Norwegian campaign, calls were made throughout the British Army for men to join the new Commando units. The first volunteers were formed into No.11 Independent Company, with an establishment of twenty-five officers and 350 other ranks. The first commando raid, **Operation Collar**, was carried out on the night of 24/25 June 1940 – a raid on the Pas de Calais. The raid's objective was the reconnaissance of four locations and the capture of prisoners. One hundred and fifteen men of No. 11 Independent Company carried out the operation. No military intelligence was gathered, nor was damage caused enemy equipment; the only success on this first commando raid was the bayoneting of two German sentries. Why were they kill when the purpose of the raid was to take prisoners? German propaganda called them *murderous thugs and cut throats who killed soldiers and civilians indiscriminately, preferring to murde their enemies rather than take prisoners.*

By the autumn of 1940 more than 2,000 men had volunteered for commando training.

812ww2/2, 813ww2/2. Recruits were trained at special centres in Scotland. They were brought to a very high level of physical fitness and were taught survival, orienteering, close-quarter combat, silent killing, signalling, amphibious and cliff assault, vehicle operation, the handling of different weapons and demolition skills.

16ww2/2 Two Royal Navy Landing Ships Infantry (LSI), HMS *Queen Emma* and HMS *Princess Beatrix*, departed from Scapa Flow, 1 March 1941, carrying men of No 3 and No 4 Commando, as well as Royal Engineer demolition experts and a contingent of fifty-two Norwegian troops. It was a three day voyage and the weather was rough.

Rear Admiral Louis Keppel Hamilton, commander of the raid.

Operation Claymore was the first large scale commando raid by the new formation, 4 March 1941. It was a landing on the Lofoten Islands, off the Norwegian coast and inside the Arctic Circle. The commandos would be landed at four ports to destroy fish oil producing factories. The oil produced was being shipped to Germany, where glycerine was extracted (an ingredient in the manufacture of high explosives). The commander of the raid was Rear Admiral Louis Keppel Hamilton. The Royal Navy was to escort the transports to the islands and back. While there, they were to destroy or capture any German shipping or Norwegian shipping working for the Germans and provide naval gunfire support for the landing forces.

817ww2/2 Providing escort for the LSI were five destroyers. HMS *Somali*, leader of the 6th Destroyer flotilla, which comprised: HMS *Bedouin*, *Tartar*, *Eskimo* and *Legion*.

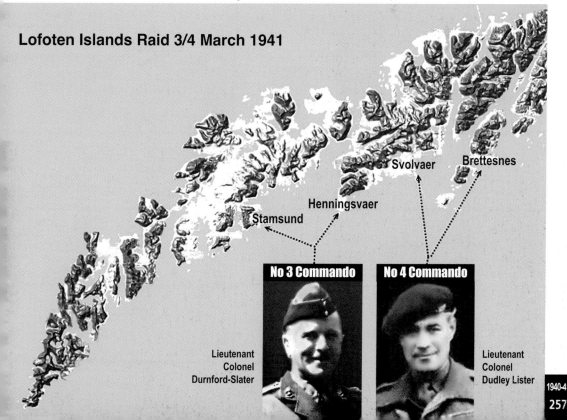

Lofoten Islands Raid 3/4 March 1941

Brettesnes

Svolvaer

Henningsvaer

Stamsund

No 3 Commando

Lieutenant Colonel Durnford-Slater

No 4 Commando

Lieutenant Colonel Dudley Lister

824ww2/2, 820ww2/2. Commandos in landing craft leaving the parent ship HMS *Princess Beatrix* and heading to the shore at dawn. Nearing the coastline, as seen from an accompanying destroyer.

As the raiders approached the islands a German armed trawler, *Krebs NN04*, was spotted sailing off Svolvaer, one of 4 Commando's designated landing areas. HMS *Somali* opened fire, hitting the wheelhouse and killing the captain and several of the crew. The vessel was disabled but stayed afloat. Later the *Somali* signals officer, Lieutenant Sir Marshall Warmington, boarded the abandoned vessel and retrieved some documents and two Enigma code machine rotors. It proved to be an important aid for the code-breakers at Bletchley Park. Five wounded German sailors were taken off before the vessel was sunk by shellfire. Out of a crew of twenty-five, eighteen were killed.

825ww2/2 German armed trawler *NN04 Krebs* of Narvik's *Hafenschutzflottille* (port protection). The trawler was attacked and later sunk by HMS *Somali* allowing vital code material to be retrieved.

827ww2/2 Corporal John Shaw, British Commandos –Lofoten raid, March 1941.

82ww2/2 Fish oil storage tanks set on fire by the engineers.

826ww2/2 German fishing boat *Lachs HH 61* was one of the vessels sunk during the commando assault on Lofoten.

818ww2/2 Stacked barrels of oil have been broken open and the contents poured into the harbour and ignited. The commandos had achieved total surprise. Locals going to work as usual believed that the presence of the armed troops was part of an elaborate German training exercise.

832ww2/2 German soldiers, (at least one is a member of the *Luftwaffe*), officials and collaborators were rounded up, blindfolded and loaded onto landing craft for the return trip to Scotland. Sixty quislings (collaborators) and 225 German prisoners were taken in the Lofoten Raid. Volunteers to join the Norwegian forces (including eight women) were also taken back with the commandos.

821ww2/2 Oil storage tanks at the fish oil refineries, factories, offices, buildings used for military purposes and ships in the harbour were systematically blown up

019ww2/2 A crowded landing craft returning to the LCIs after the first successful commando raid. The only Allied casualty was a leg wound caused by an officer accidently shooting himself with his revolver.

031ww2/2 On the return trip a Norwegian prisoner, a 'quisling'collaborator with the Nazis, under guard on HMS *Princess Beatrix*, doubtless is considering his future as a captive traitor in England. He seems to be eyeing up the Tommy gun, but the magazine has been removed.

The Germans had been caught unprepared and the landings were unopposed. Within an hour the commandos had taken all their objectives. The raid was a success: eleven fish oil factories and storage tanks were destroyed; ten ships sunk, 225 prisoners taken and with an unknown number of German sailors killed on the sunken ships. An added bonus for the Allies were the 315 Norwegian volunteers brought back to join the Free Norwegian Forces.

030ww2/2 Rear Admiral Louis Keppel Hamilton, commander of the raid, on the return journey aboard HMS *Somali*.

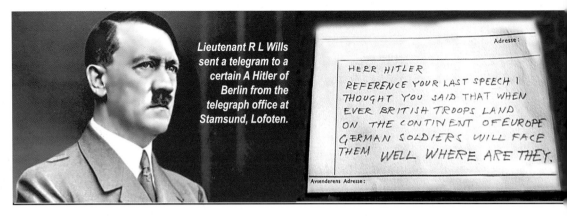

Lieutenant R L Wills sent a telegram to a certain A Hitler of Berlin from the telegraph office at Stamsund, Lofoten.

HERR HITLER
REFERENCE YOUR LAST SPEECH I
THOUGHT YOU SAID THAT WHEN
EVER BRITISH TROOPS LAND
ON THE CONTINENT OF EUROPE
GERMAN SOLDIERS WILL FACE
THEM WELL WHERE ARE THEY.

Operation Claymore was the first of twelve Allied attacks on Norwegian soil – four of them in 1941.
Hitler would have to employ serious numbers of men to defend his occupation of Norway.

40ww2/2 A British flying column sent to meet Soviet troops came together near Kavzin, Iran. The Russian armoured car is a GAZ.BA-10 with a .5 mm gun.

Chapter Ten: **Churchill Joins Hands With Stalin – Iran**

43ww2/2 Defeated without a shot, a scene typical of many throughout Iran in late August and early September 1941: soldiers of a disarmed and isbanded Iranian Army formation watch as British and Soviet forces take over their country. Armed resistance would have been a pointless waste.

850ww2/2 British troops viewing the city of Baghdad, 11 June 1941.

The Anglo–Iraqi War, 2–31 May 1941; this was a British military campaign against Iraq that preceded the Anglo-Soviet invasion of Iran. The Iraq government under Rashid Ali had seized power during the Second World War with assistance from Germany and Italy. The British military campaign resulted in the downfall of Rashid Ali's government, the re-occupation of Iraq by the British and the return to power of the Regent of Iraq, Prince Abd al-Ilah, an ally to imperial Britain.

851ww2/2 Rashid Ali al-Gaylani, Prime Minister of Iraq. He was an Arab nationalist who attempted to remove the British influence from Iraq. During his brief tenures as Prime Minister in 1940 and 1941, he tried to negotiate settlements with the Axis powers in order to counter British influence in Iraq. Britain responded with severe economic sanctions against the country.

849ww2/2 The Iranian warship *Babr* (Tiger) after being sunk by HMAS *Yarra* during the surprise attack on Iran in August 1941 (no declaration of war had been made).

During August, HMAS *Yarra* (Australian Navy) operated in Iranian waters in support of the Anglo-Soviet invasion. The *Yarra* secured several ports and oil-producing facilities and sank the sloop *Babr*. She was also involved in the capture of two Iranian gunboats. HMAS *Yarra* was later sunk by a Japanese cruiser force south of Java on 4 March 1942.

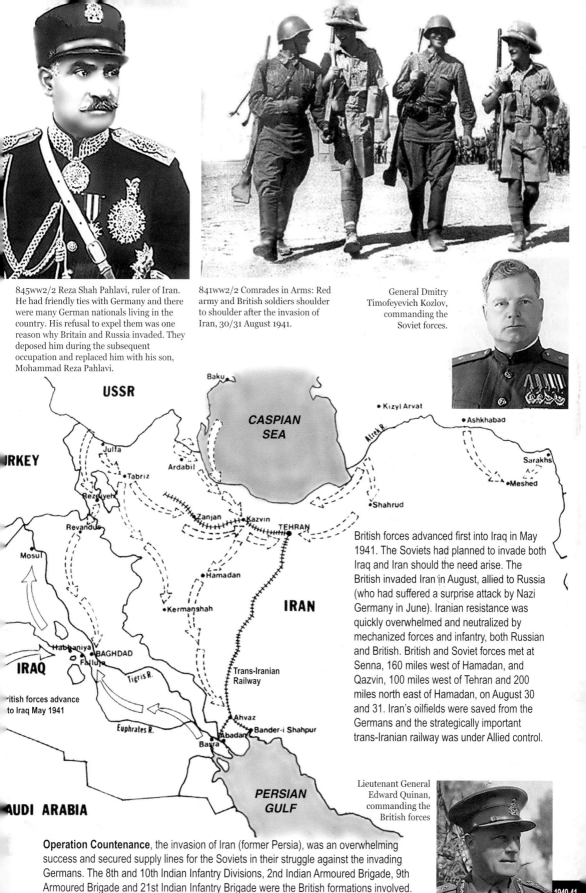

845ww2/2 Reza Shah Pahlavi, ruler of Iran. He had friendly ties with Germany and there were many German nationals living in the country. His refusal to expel them was one reason why Britain and Russia invaded. They deposed him during the subsequent occupation and replaced him with his son, Mohammad Reza Pahlavi.

841ww2/2 Comrades in Arms: Red army and British soldiers shoulder to shoulder after the invasion of Iran, 30/31 August 1941.

General Dmitry Timofeyevich Kozlov, commanding the Soviet forces.

British forces advanced first into Iraq in May 1941. The Soviets had planned to invade both Iraq and Iran should the need arise. The British invaded Iran in August, allied to Russia (who had suffered a surprise attack by Nazi Germany in June). Iranian resistance was quickly overwhelmed and neutralized by mechanized forces and infantry, both Russian and British. British and Soviet forces met at Senna, 160 miles west of Hamadan, and Qazvin, 100 miles west of Tehran and 200 miles north east of Hamadan, on August 30 and 31. Iran's oilfields were saved from the Germans and the strategically important trans-Iranian railway was under Allied control.

Lieutenant General Edward Quinan, commanding the British forces

Operation Countenance, the invasion of Iran (former Persia), was an overwhelming success and secured supply lines for the Soviets in their struggle against the invading Germans. The 8th and 10th Indian Infantry Divisions, 2nd Indian Armoured Brigade, 9th Armoured Brigade and 21st Indian Infantry Brigade were the British formations involved.

855ww2/2 Inspection of troops prior to the Joint Russo-British military parade in Tehran, September 1941.

857ww2/2 The trans-Iranian railway taking vital supplies to aid the Soviet forces in the struggle against the Axis invading armies. Around a thousand German nationals had been operating the trans-Iranian railway system. It was the Shah's government's failure to heed the Allies insistance that they be evicted that prompted the occupation of the nation.

856ww2/2 Soviet six horse foot artillery team, on the streets of Tabriz during the occupation.

844ww2/2 Two soldiers of the Indian army guarding the Abadan Refinery in Iran, 4 September 1941.

852ww2/2 Reza Shah Pahlavi appealed to the President of the USA to intervene to stop the invasion by Britain and Russia.

854ww2/2 On 17 September 1941 Mohammad Reza was inaugurated as Shah of Iran.

853ww2/2 Franklin D Roosevelt.

The Shah sent a telegram to the American President, Franklin D Roosevelt, pleading with him to stop the invasion. However, as the neutral United States had nothing to do with the attack, Roosevelt was not able to respond to the Shah's plea, other than stating that he believed that the 'territorial integrity' of Iran should be respected. On 16 September 1941, it was announced that Reza Shah had resigned (deposed) and that his son, twenty-one year old Mohammad Reza, was to replace him.

Where next?